TAPHONOMY:
A Bibliographic Guide to the Literature

TAPHONOMY:
A Bibliographic Guide to the Literature

COMPILED BY:
Christopher P. Koch

PEOPLING OF THE AMERICAS PUBLICATIONS
Bibliographic Series

CENTER FOR THE STUDY OF THE FIRST AMERICANS
Institute for Quaternary Studies
University of Maine
Orono, Maine

TAPHONOMY: A Bibliographic Guide to the Literature
©1989 Center for the Study of the First Americans. All rights reserved.
No part of this book may be reproduced, projected, stored in a retrieval system, or transmitted, for whatever purpose, in any form or by any means, whether electronic, mechanical, magnetic, photographic, laser, or otherwise, without the prior written permission of the publisher: Center for the Study of the First Americans, 495 College Avenue, University of Maine, Orono, ME 04473.

Printed in the United States of America

ISBN: 0-912933-05-4

THE CENTER FOR THE STUDY OF THE FIRST AMERICANS

The Center for the Study of the First Americans is an affiliate of the Institute for Quaternary Studies and the Department of Anthropology at the University of Maine. It was established in July 1981 by a seed grant from Mr. William Bingham's Trust for Charity. The Center's goals are to encourage research about Pleistocene peoples of the Americas, and to make this new knowledge available to both the scientific community and the interested public. Toward this end, the Center staff is developing research, public outreach, and publications programs.

The Center's *Peopling of the Americas* publication program focuses on the earliest Americans and their environments. This program includes: (1) a monograph series presenting primary data on sites in North and South America which are more than 10,000 years old; (2) a process series presenting new methods and theories for interpreting early remains; (3) an edited volume series presenting topical papers and symposia proceedings; (4) a popular book series making the most significant discoveries and research available to the general public; and (5) a bibliographic series.

In addition, the Center publishes a quarterly newspaper called the *Mammoth Trumpet*. The newspaper is written for both a general and a professional audience. The Center also published an annual journal, *Current Research in the Pleistocene*. The journal presents note-length articles about current research in the interdisciplinary field of Quaternary studies as they relate to the field of the Pleistocene peopling of the Americas.

MANUSCRIPT SUBMISSIONS

BOOKS

The Center solicits high-quality original manuscripts in English. For information write to: Robson Bonnichsen, Center for the Study of the First Americans, 495 College Avenue, Orono, ME 04473.

CURRENT RESEARCH IN THE PLEISTOCENE

Researchers wishing to submit summaries in this annual serial should contact editor Jim I. Mead, Department of Geology, Northern Arizona University, Box 666, Flagstaff, AZ 80811 or request Information for Contributors from the Center. The deadline for submissions is January 31 of each calendar year; early submission is suggested.

MAMMOTH TRUMPET

News of discoveries, reports on recent conferences, book reviews and news of current issues are invited. Contact editor Karen L. Turnmire at the Center.

ADDITIONALLY . . .

Authors are encouraged to submit reprints of published articles or copies of unpublished papers for inclusion in the Center's research library. Exchanges of relevant books and periodicals with other publishers is also encouraged. Please address contributions and correspondence to the Center's library.

PEOPLING OF THE AMERICAS PUBLICATIONS

OTHER TITLES

UNDERSTANDING STONE TOOLS: A COGNITIVE APPROACH
David E. Young and Robson Bonnichsen
ISBN: 0-912933-00-3

ARCHAEOLOGICAL SEDIMENTS IN CONTEXT
Julie K. Stein and William R. Farrand, Editors
ISBN: 0-912933-01-1

ENVIRONMENTS AND EXTINCTIONS:
MAN IN LATE GLACIAL NORTH AMERICA
Jim I. Mead and David J. Meltzer, Editors
ISBN: 0-912933-02-x

NEW EVIDENCE FOR THE PLEISTOCENE PEOPLING OF THE AMERICAS
Contributions in English, Spanish, and Portuguese with extensive English abstracts
Alan L. Bryan, Editor
ISBN: 0-912933-03-8

BONE MODIFICATION
Published proceedings of the First International Bone Modification Conference
Robson Bonnichsen and Marcella H. Sorg, Editors
ISBN: 0-912033-06-2

Contents

Acknowledgements ix

Introduction 1

Bibliographic Entries 7

Author Index 51

Key Word Index 61

Acknowledgments

The publication of this bibliography would have been impossible without the cooperation and help of many individuals who are far too numerous to mention. Nevertheless, I will try to remember them all. I am indebted to Rob Bonnichsen, Marcella Sorg, Earlene Hinton and Judith Cooper of the Center for the Study of the First Americans at the University of Maine. These people and their staff undertook the arduous task of shepherding this bibliography through production and into print.

Rob Bonnichsen, Andrew Hill and Achilles Gautier contributed substantial amounts of time and effort to this work over the years. Rob Bonnichsen, the Center's director, made the original commitment to publish this bibliography and has stuck by us all through what has turned into a very long editorial process.

Earlene Hinton was primarily responsible for establishing a uniform bibliographic format, used herein. She, Barbara Harrity and Janis Pendleton verified most of the periodical and monograph titles. John Sherblom, University of Maine Computing and Processing Service, Jim Fastook, University of Maine Computer Science Department, and Terry Kelly, University of Maine Printing Office helped with the computer work.

Special thanks must go to Jean Keller and Stella Gora of the Professors Book Delivery Service, and to Margret Byrne of the Interlibrary Loan Department, all from the Erindale College Library, University of Toronto. Thanks are also due the staff of the Raymond H. Fogler Library at the University of Maine, particularly to Evelyn Dearborn, Head of Cataloguing, and Carol Curtis and Dottie Hutchins of the Interlibrary Loan Department. This bibliography would have been impossible without the help of these expert librarians and their staffs.

At the Center for the Study of the First Americans, the following people have helped with data entry and other unpleasant tasks: Maria Fuentes, Karen Hudgins, Janis Pendleton and Barbara Harrity.

Over the years the following people have contributed references, publications, help and advice: J.W. Bailey, A.K. Behrensmeyer, D. Berg, R. Bonnichsen, H.T. Bunn, T.Y. Canby, G.H. Cole, D.E. Dechant-Boaz, A. Gautier, D.P. Gifford-Gonzalez, B.C. Gordon, C.B. Hanson, C.R. Harington, G.A. Haynes, A.P. Hill, W.N. Irving, G.L. Isaac, M. Jackes, A.V. Jopling, C. Junker-Andersen, M.A. Katzenburg, W.W. Korth, J.W. Kitching, R.G. Klein, F.R. Lisowski, R.L. Lyman, J.E. McArdle, R.E. Morlan, N. Noe-Nygaard, D.R. Pilbeam, L.A. Pavlish, S. Payne, R.B. Potts, W.C. Rodriguez, E. Shakeri, M. Skinner, P.L. Shipman, S. Stallibrass, L.G. Straus, J. Tomenchuk, H. Toots, E. Trinkaus, K. Valoch and E.S. Vrba.

C. K.
1988

Introduction

A Note to Users

I started this bibliography a little over a decade ago. Because of my involvement at that time with Bonnichsen's research on Upper Pleistocene bone modification at Old Crow (Yukon Territory, Canada), this bibliography originally dealt with early hominid bone modification. Working on this project, I began to realize that there were a host of other processes that could, and often did, alter bone in a manner similar to that attributed to hominids. Clearly, then, in order to understand the role hominids played in accumulating and modifying bones one must have an appreciation of the other biological and geological processes that act on faunal remains. This work is the natural outgrowth of library research into all the various processes that contribute to the accumulation, modification, destruction, and preservation of archaeological and paleontological remains.

For the purpose of this bibliography, taphonomy is defined in its broadest possible sense. Within this broad definition, taphonomy is interdisciplinary. It is not just restricted to the study of bones and fossils, but includes the taphonomy of stone artifacts and other archaeological as well as biological and geological remains.

The literature relevant to the study of taphonomy is widely dispersed across disciplinary boundaries and can be difficult to locate. The goal of this bibliography is to aid both the new student and the experienced professional in their taphonomic research, whether it is of an archaeological, paleoanthropological, paleontological, or paleoecological nature. Although emphasis is on sources in archaeology and paleoanthropology, I hope this guide will enable researchers from many fields to take advantage of this large and rapidly expanding body of information.

The photocopied first version of this work was circulated to colleagues in 1979. It was so well received that I decided to try to keep it up to date. As the bibliography began to grow, it became apparent that indexing was required. Early attempts at assigning key words to each entry were of limited success, due to a lack of consistency in the choice of key words. In the 1980s, with the help of the staff at the Center for the Study of the First Americans, these difficulties were largely overcome. I chose the key words for all entries, and any citations I could not inspect personally were not included. Users are strongly urged to read through the index before using the bibliography.

Bibliographic entries are indexed in two ways: by author or authors, and by key words. The computer program allowed each entry to have up to six key words; each of the six key words could have two modifiers. Index entries were, for the most part, chosen to reflect taphonomic processes, for example abrasion, butchery, carnivore modification, fossilization etc. When a book or article covered a range of topics, I indexed only the taphonomically relevant portions.

This work includes entries published before the end of 1987. The one exception to this rule is the forthcoming collection of articles entitled *Bone Modification* being published by the Center for the Study of the First Americans. I located most of the sources in this bibliography by examining literature cited in known works. I also monitored current periodicals in general science, anthropology, archaeology, paleontology, and geology. Several researchers active in the field sent reprints and hard-to-get items. No attempt was made to systematically check periodical indexes, although they were consulted on occasion. This work is by no means complete, and I would invite users to send me material I have overlooked.

Titles of journals, serials, conference proceedings, and publication series were checked by E. Hinton in standard references such as the *National Union Catalogue* (*NUC*), the *Union List of Serials* (*NLS*), or *New Serial Titles* (*NST*). All but a small number have been verified. The more obscure monographs were double-checked in the *NUC* or equivalent sources. All works cited in this introduction can be found in the bibliography.

The bibliographic style conforms almost entirely with the *American Antiquity* style sheet. The exceptions to this are serial titles, publication series, and published conference proceedings. The rules for these publications are a variant of those used by most libraries in North America. By making the entries substantially congruent with major reference sources (*NUC*, *ULS*, *NST*) and databases (OCLC), I hope that the lives of researchers and interlibrary loan librarians will be made a little easier.

A Brief History of Taphonomy

Today taphonomy is recognized as an integral component of archaeozoology, paleoanthropology, paleontology, and paleobotany. Research reports in these fields are considered incomplete without some discussion of the taphonomic history of the collection. Archaeologists and paleoanthropologists rely on taphonomic analysis to provide them with biological, geological, and cultural information. Traditionally, biological and geological information has been used to make inferences about the paleoecology of the site. This information may provide clues to the mode of accumulation of an assemblage. Cultural information gleaned from taphonomic studies can help us answer questions concerning prehistoric behavior, such as the technology of bone modification, and the subsistence base and social behavior of past cultures.

A brief history of the broad and expanding field of taphonomy can hardly do justice to this rich body of literature. This historical outline is intended to highlight some of the more important research trends in taphonomy and emphasize how these trends have shaped thinking in anthropological archaeology. I hope that this history will be of use to those unfamiliar with taphonomy and will stimulate them to read the original sources. Those who are interested in a more detailed treatment of the history of taphonomy are urged to consult Hill (1970 or 1978), Olson (1980, 1985), Dodson (1980), Gifford (1982), Binford (1981, 1985), and Behrensmeyer and Kidwell (1985). Users who are new to the field of taphonomy will find that Shipman's (1981b) introductory book is a useful guide.

For most of this century, researchers have been conducting studies relevant to the field of taphonomy. Today many archaeologists, confronted with faunal data analyzed from a taphonomic perspective, are unaware of the foundations of this approach. This bibliography is intended to serve as a bridge between the several disciplines that are involved with modern taphonomic research, to help outline and explain this multidisciplinary approach. The introduction tries to define taphonomy and briefly trace its development. It also highlights some of the achievements of taphonomy, and speculates on the goals and objectives of the field as they are relevant to anthropological archaeology and paleoanthropology.

Taphonomy has been defined by several people and in many ways. My favorite definition, coined by Peter Dodson (1980:6), surmises that "[t]aphonomy is a subject fit for burial." A more detailed definition of taphonomy views it as a process or chain of events that begins just before the death of an organism, and proceeds through decomposition, disarticulation, burial, fossilization, exposure, and collection. At each stage of this process, various taphonomic agencies intervene to obscure, bias, and add to the information that is available from the resulting collection (Koch 1986).

Origins and Early History of Taphonomy

The term taphonomy was introduced by Soviet paleontologist I.A. Efremov (1940). Composed of the Greek words for burial *(taphos)* and law *(nomos)*, taphonomy may be defined simply as the laws of burial. Efremov was interested in establishing generalizations or laws of taphonomy and he intended it to be:

> the study of the transformation (in all its details) of animal remains from the biosphere into the litho-sphere, i.e., the study of the process in the upshot of which the organisms pass out of the different parts of the biosphere and, being fossilized, become part of the lithosphere (Efremov 1940:85).

Essentially, Efremov believed taphonomy was the study of the processes involved in information loss. Current taphonomic research, in addition to studying postmortem information loss, has focused on the ways in which information is added to and transformed in the fossil record. In recognition of this expansion, Behrensmeyer and Kidwell proposed the following, broader definition of taphonomy: "... the study of the processes of preservation and how they affect information in the fossil record" (Behrensmeyer and Kidwell 1985:105). This definition, like many others, arises from the field of paleontology and does not take into account the complexities of hominid cultural practices. Archaeologists and paleoanthropologists may find it more useful to restate this definition as the study of the processes of preservation and modification, and how they affect geological, biological, and cultural information in the geological record.

Taphonomic research grew out of attempts by paleontologists to reconstruct paleocommunities, and hence paleoenvironments. Hill articulated this point well when he stated that

> [t]aphonomy ultimately deals with the differences that exist between an assemblage, or collection, and the community or communities of animals from which they come (Hill 1978:88).

Most paleontologists agree with this statement and consider taphonomy to be complementary to the study of paleoecology (Olson 1962; Lawrence 1968; Voorhies 1969).

The taphonomic heritage that archaeologists and paleoanthropologists share derives from two distinct traditions: paleontology (vertebrate and invertebrate) and geology; and archaeology. Evolving parallel to each other since the beginning of the 20th century, it was not until the late 1970s that these traditions began to be synthesized in an anthropologically meaningful way.

The Paleontological Tradition

Early in the 20th century, paleontologists and natural scientists began to realize that the fossil assemblages they studied were not true representations of the living communities from which they derived. In time it was understood that the transformation of members of a biological community into a fossil assemblage was a complex and destructive process. German paleontologists were among the first to investigate these postmortem events. Wasmund (1926) pointed out that animals that died in the same area did not necessarily originate in the same community or habitat. To better understand the destructive roles of decomposition, disarticulation, fluvial transport, and burial, Weigelt (1927) studied mass drownings of cows and other vertebrates. He termed his work "biostratinomy" and intended it to treat postmortem transformation of animal remains (see Seilacher 1973).

German paleontologists made a number of important contributions to the field of taphonomy throughout this century. Early on, German paleontologists developed the tradition of actuopaleontology (Richter 1928; Gifford 1982). The basic premises of actuopaleontology are: that destructive processes are uniformitarian in nature, and that studies of living and recently dead organisms can shed light on the postmortem histories of fossil assemblages. This tradition, often termed actualism or neotaphonomy, continues today. Much of this research has been translated into English, the most comprehensive of which is Schafer's (1977) study of North Sea marine communities. A later contribution to the study of taphonomy is the development of the working group *Sonderforschungsbereich* 53 (SFB). This group, integrating the research of paleontologists, geologists, botanists, zoologists, geochemists, mineralogists, anthropologists, and archaeologists, appears to be one of the most ambitious attempts made to study all of the facets of taphonomy.

The research conducted during this early period lacked a theoretical framework that could unify postmortem events with later diagenetic processes. This framework was provided by Efremov. He believed that taphonomy was the discipline that would unify paleontology, biology, and geology, "into one general geo-biological historical method of study (1940:93)." Efremov (1958) reasoned that there is a dialectical relationship between the reconstruction of paleocommunities and the destructive processes that have acted upon them. Because he wrote in Russian and his 1940 article was published in an obscure English-language journal, Efremov's work was initially less influential in the English-speaking world than that of his German colleagues.

North American paleontologists became aware of Efremov's work primarily through the writings of Olson (1957, 1962), who translated several of Efremov's works into English. Olson also drew the attention of North Americans to the postmortem damage skeletal assemblages undergo, and he was one of the first to systematically model taphonomic events and agencies.

Following its introduction by Olson, taphonomy slowly infiltrated North American paleontology. Taphonomic research in paleontology, at this time, was split between the study of marine and terrestrial environments. Invertebrate and vertebrate research proceeded independently, often resulting in the duplication of research (Olson 1980).

Most early taphonomic research was conducted by invertebrate paleontologists. Miyadi and Habe (1947) examined recent death assemblages from Japanese bays. Boucot (1953) compared the age structure of living mollusk communities with that of death assemblages. Johnson (1957), in an actualist study, investigated the burial of shells. Gifford (1982) has pointed out that most studies at this time were concerned with the relationship between postmortem processes and the results observed in the fossil record. Several studies concentrated on actualist as well as experimental work in an attempt to understand this relationship. Excellent examples of this type of research can be seen in studies of shell abrasion (Boucot 1953; Driscoll 1967; Driscoll and Weltin 1973), breakage (Boyd and Newell 1972; Trewin and Welsh 1972), and aqueous transport and burial (Menard and Boucot 1951; Boucot, Brace, and DeMar 1958; Larson 1977; Trewin and Welsh 1972).

Among vertebrate paleontologists, Shotwell (1955, 1958) tried to link animal habitat preferences with the relative abundance of recovered fossil taxa. Clark et al. (1967), building on the work of Olson, presented perhaps the best statement of the systematic approach to taphonomic studies in their classic paper on the Oligocene vertebrates of North Dakota. This model, in one form or another, figures prominently in the introductions of most general texts on taphonomy.

In North America, Voorhies's (1969) work with Pliocene vertebrates from the western United States, and Dodson's (19??) research on Upper Cretaceous reptiles from western Canada are among the earliest paleontological studies in taphonomy. By drawing attention to the importance of fluvial processes in amassing and dispersing fossil assemblages, these works stimulated further study of these processes. Behrensmeyer (1975a), in her study of the vertebrates from the hominid-bearing Koobi Fora Formation in Kenya, demonstrated that fossils can be studied using the same parameters employed with other sedimentary particles. Hill (1975; Hill and Walker 1972) initiated an actualistic study in several different Ugandan environments to better understand the fate of the bones of recently dead animals.

Through paleontology and the work of Behrensmeyer and Hill, taphonomic research became a part of paleoanthropology, where, at this time, it was used to help explain paleoecological issues. The works of Behrensmeyer and Hill greatly stimulated taphonomic research in early hominid studies. In 1976, with the aid of the Wenner-Gren Foundation for Anthropological Research, they organized the first English-language symposium on taphonomy. This interdisciplinary gathering, entitled "Taphonomy and Vertebrate Paleoecology" brought together experts in most aspects of taphonomic research. This symposium and the subsequent publication of the symposium papers brought taphonomy to the attention of archaeologists worldwide.

The Archaeological Tradition

If taphonomy was slow to influence North American paleontology, it was even slower to influence prehistoric research. It was not until the late 1970s that most prehistorians became cognizant of the advances in taphonomy that were being made in paleontology. Archaeologists began to consider cultural usage of faunal remains as a taphonomic agency. Recognizing these cultural practices as taphonomic agencies allowed archaeologists to view bone modification within the larger framework of biological and geological bone damage.

The few studies conducted in the first decade of this century by archaeologists and paleoanthropologists had little impact. Perhaps the first paleoanthropologists to conduct taphonomic research were Duckworth and Dubois. Dubois's discoveries of *Pithecanthropus erectus* on the island of Java created great controversy. Dubois contended the rather primitive-looking skull cap was associated with a robust but modern looking femur, although the two were found 15 meters apart on the banks of the Solo River. He suggested that crocodiles had dispersed the bones (Dubois 1927). As Duckworth (1904:274) pointed out, ". . . it is very important, if not essential, for Dr. Dubois' theory that the two bones should be regarded as having formed part of the same skeleton." To solve this dilemma, Duckworth made observations on a horse skeleton that had been scattered by a small stream in Carnarvonshire, U.K. He found that a stream smaller than the Solo River was capable of separating the humeri by 47 meters.

Contemporaneously with Duckworth's research, studies of prehistoric bone technology were being conducted in France using the Upper Paleolithic bone tools that were being recovered in large numbers. Martin (1910) carried out what may have been the first experimental study into hominid bone breakage patterns when he broke bones of several large animals and reported on the resulting fractures. Several other French archaeologists studied broken and worked bone (see Mercier 1935; Octobon, Begouen, and Begouen 1935; Begouen and Begouen 1937), and Breuil (1932, 1938) began to formulate his ideas regarding the use of bone tools in the Lower Paleolithic. Breuil's ideas had far-reaching effects in archaeology and continued to dominate archaeological studies of faunal remains until the 1970s.

Perhaps the best known early taphonomic studies conducted by prehistorians were those of Pei (1938) and Breuil (1939). When the remains of Peking Man were unearthed from Zhoukoudian so were thousands of animal bones. Most of these bones were fragmentary, and several bore incisions and other forms of damage. Two theories evolved to interpret these remains. One, championed by Pei, maintained that the damage was caused by animals and natural geological processes. The other theory, as proposed by Breuil, held that the remains represented an extensive bone and antler tool industry. Breuil's explanation was more attractive to an imaginative scientific community and had the larger number of proponents. The debate continues today (see Binford and Ho 1985; Binford and Stone 1986). Another important aspect of Breuil's research was his realization that fresh, dried, and fossil bones exhibit different fracture patterns and morphologies. His work directly influenced Dart as well as later researchers (see Bonnichsen 1979; Johnson 1983). Although Duckworth, Dubois, Pei, and Breuil pioneered taphonomic studies in prehistoric research, it was Raymond Dart who stimulated contemporary taphonomic research in archaeology and, to a large degree, paleoanthropology as well.

In addition to trying to convince the scientific community that australopithecines were indeed human ancestors, Dart also focused his attention on the faunal remains associated with them. At Makapansgat, Dart (1957) believed he had found evidence of an extensive bone, tooth, and horn (osteodontokeratic) tool industry. Accepting the earlier work of Breuil, he believed that fresh bone breaks differently than dry or fossil bone. Dart theorized that australopithecines cracked long bones then twisted them to produce long spiraling fractures. He believed a long bone fractured in this manner was suitable for use as a weapon or tool. Upon analyzing the faunal remains, Dart discovered that several bones and bone parts were present in unexpected frequencies. The distal ends of humeri, for example, outnumbered proximal ends. Certain bones (e.g., caudal vertebra) were virtually absent. Dart attributed this differential preservation to the actions of early hominids. The humerus with its proximal end removed made a formidable weapon; tails (caudal vertebra) could be used as whips and signals. While his ideas may sound farfetched today, they stimulated his critics to seek alternative explanations (i.e., Washburn 1957; Brain 1981). It was this search for more suitable explanations that prompted many archaeologists to begin to question the nature of faunal accumulations.

Much of the research into origins of faunal assemblages involved the search for diagnostic criteria that would distinguish between hominid cultural behavior and other agents of bone accumulation. Bonnichsen (1973, 1979) used an approach borrowed from lithic analysis and began to investigate the material properties of bone. Building on the work of Breuil, he demonstrated that bone fractures in different ways depending on its material state (fresh, dry, or fossilized). Because as fresh bone dries and becomes fossilized its material state changes, the resulting fracture surface morphologies differ. Bonnichsen (1979) applied this approach to the controversial Upper Pleistocene fauna from Old Crow. Whether Bonnichsen was correct in his assertion that this bone breakage was the product of cultural behavior is still in contention. Bonnichsen was, however, one of the first archaeologists to view cultural behavior as a taphonomic factor and to voice that view with in the theoretical framework of taphonomy.

At roughly the same time, a group of Africanist archaeologists, working under the influence of Isaac, were also beginning to bring an archaeological perspective to taphonomic research. Isaac (1967) had conducted research into bone weathering, disarticulation, and scattering in the contemporary East African environment. Because of his association with the Koobi Fora Research Project, Isaac and his students had access to the ongoing work of Behrensmeyer and Hill.

An Anthropological Synthesis

The developments in taphonomic research of the late 1970s and early 1980s gave rise to a synthesis of paleontological and archaeological methods and theory. This synthesis has transformed traditional taphonomy into a broad theoretical framework that is more congruent with anthropological archaeology.

North American research tended to concentrate on the delineation of parameters for the agents of bone breakage or modification (i.e., Frison 1978; Morlan 1980; Haynes 1981; Binford and Bertram 1977; Binford 1978, 1981; Johnson 1983). This work was founded, for the most part, in a technological approach to bone modification. At the same time, the efforts of paleoanthropologists had their roots in paleoecology (i.e., Shipman 1977; Behrensmeyer and Dechant 1980; Badgley 1982; Dechant-Boaz 1982). Brain (1970, 1976, 1978, 1981) was an exception to this trend. He concentrated on the agents responsible for the South African cave accumulations—in this case leopards and other cats. Gifford's (1977; Gifford and Behrensmeyer 1977) work was also an exception; it contributed to the taphonomy of site formation processes.

Archaeology students influenced by Isaac and exposed to the ideas embodied in the "New Archaeology" (as espoused by Binford) followed the lead of Brain and Gifford-Gonzalez. The result of this initiative was a series of studies that dealt with the agents responsible for site formation processes (Gifford 1977; Bunn 1982; Potts 1982). It is interesting to note that these anthropologists, aware of the work of North American archaeologists, began to consider the technological properties of bone in their research. It is likely that these considerations were responsible for many of the bone damage studies (Bunn 1981; Shipman, Besler, and Davis 1981) and microscopic analyses of cut-marked bones (Bunn 1981; Potts and Shipman; Shipman 1981a) being published at the time.

Interest in taphonomy has continued to grow at a phenomenal rate. This interest also has had a tremendous impact on research in archaeozoology and anthropological archaeology. I would like to examine briefly some of the ways in which taphonomy, especially anthropologically oriented taphonomy, has contributed to our understanding of information contained in the past.

The first and most obvious contribution of taphonomy is to the field of paleoecology. Taphonomic studies have led to the derivation of more accurate environmental information from fossil hominid sites. This information has yielded valuable clues to the adaptive strategies of the early hominids (see Behrensmeyer 1975b). A second, and often overlooked, contribution has been made regarding cultural information. Increasingly common use of taphonomic analysis has led to a closer examination of the means of bone accumulation, especially where bones are associated with stone tools. It is no longer acceptable to attribute this association automatically to cultural practices (see Binford 1981, 1985; Isaac 1983; Koch 1986). Studies of bone technology and hominid modification not only aid the identification of the means of bone accumulation, but they also shed light on tool-use activity and feeding behavior.

Taphonomy has not only provided insight into bone technology and the means of bone accumulation, but it also has added to our understanding of prehistoric subsistence strategies. Dart's view of early hominids as mighty hunters and cannibals has been replaced by a humbler opinion of our ancestors. The increased reliance on taphonomic analysis is partly responsible for this changed view. The subsistence base of early hominids is amenable to several forms of taphonomic analysis. New techniques, such as electron microscopy, have been employed to differentiate cutmarks made by hominids from other sources of damage. These studies indicate that hominids may have begun meat-eating as scavengers rather than hunters (Binford 1981). The study of butchery patterns has produced valuable information on meat processing techniques in different cultures. Archaeologists now are able to estimate the amount of meat that could be expected from a faunal assemblage.

The central task of anthropological archaeology is to make predictions about past cultural behavior. Social relations are among the most difficult past behaviors to predict. In this area, as well, taphonomy has made a contribution. Based on his work at early archaeological sites, particularly FxJj50 in the Koobi Fora Formation (see Bunn et al.), Isaac has speculated that early hominids engaged in food sharing, food transport, and base camp living. Isaac hypothesized that sites containing voluminous bone and stone tools are occupation sites (see Isaac 1971). His interpretations, however, have been subjected to a great deal of scrutiny (see Binford 1985).

Taphonomic analysis can contribute to our understanding of the distribution of faunal remains within an archaeological site. Encountering uneven distribution of artifacts or other remains within a site, archaeologists can use taphonomic analysis to hypothesize differential site use. Taphonomic analysis also may provide insights into the darker side of human nature. Roper (1969), examining bone damage, surveyed the evidence for intrahuman violence in the Pleistocene.

From this brief history, it is obvious that taphonomy has made significant contributions to our knowledge of the past. A broader application of taphonomic procedures in the future will continue to benefit paleontology and archaeology. Additional research is needed that concentrates on the two basic taphonomic approaches: detailed studies of individual paleontological and archaeological assemblages; and explorations of the contemporary (actualistic or neotaphonomic) processes that produce the geological and archaeological record. Once we have more carefully documented collections, and we understand the processes involved in their deposition, transformation, and recovery, we can begin to address the question of whether we are on the verge of discovering the rules or laws of taphonomy as Efremov had envisaged.

Christopher P. Koch
Nairobi, Kenya, 1989

Bibliographic Entries

1. Abbie, A. A.
   1952 Incised Bones. *Australian Journal of Science* 14: 131.
2. Adams, J.
   1979 Wear of Unsound Pebbles in River Headwaters. *Science* 203: 171-172.
3. Ager, D. V.
   1963 *Paleoecology*. McGraw-Hill, New York.
4. Agenbroad, L. D.
   1989 Spiral Fractured Mammoth Bone from Non-Human Taphonomic Processes at Hot Springs, South Dakota. In *Bone Modification*, edited by R. Bonnichsen and M. Sorg (1st International Bone Modification Conference, Proceedings). Center for the Study of the First Americans, Orono, Maine.
5. Agogino, G. A., and W. O. Frankforter
   1960 A Paleo-Indian Bison Kill in Northwestern Iowa. *American Antiquity* 25: 414-415.
6. Aigner, J. S.
   1985 Comment on Binford and Ho 1985 (Reply by Binford and Ho). *Current Anthropology* 26: 429-430.
7. Aigner, J. S.
   1986 Comment on Binford and Stone 1986. *Current Anthropology* 27: 468-469.
8. Aigner, T., H. Hagdorn, and R. Mundlos
   1978 Biohermal, Biostromal and Storm-generated Coquinas in the Upper Muschelkalk. *Neues Jahrbuch für Geologie und Paläontologie. Abhandlungen* 157: 42-52.
9. Akopyan, M. M.
   1953 Syudvba Tryupov Syuslikov v Stepi. (The Fate of Corpses of Ground Squirrels (susliks) on the Steppe). *Zoologicheskii Zhurnal* 32: 1014-1019.
10. Alexander, A. K.
    1957 Bone Carrying by a Porcupine. *South African Journal of Science* 52: 257-258.
11. Alexandersson, E. T.
    1978 Destructive Diagenesis of Carbonate Sediments in the Eastern Skagerrak, North Sea. *Geology* 6: 324-327.
12. Alexandersson, E. T.
    1979 Marine Maceration of Skeletal Carbonates in the Skagerrak, North Sea. *Sedimentology* 26: 845-852.
13. Aliev, F. F.
    1972 Cases of Mass Mortality of Nutria in the Wetlands of Azerbaidzhan in Winter 1971-1972. *Mammalia* 36: 539-540.
14. Alimen, M. -H.
    1985 Comment on Binford and Ho 1985 (Reply by Binford and Ho). *Current Anthropology* 26: 430-431.
15. Aliyev, O. B.
    1978 Pereotlozhenie Okameneloctei v Verkhnemelovykh Otlozheniyakj Malogo, Kavkaza Azerbaidzhanskaya SSR (The Redeposition of Index Fossils in Upper Cretaceous Deposits of the Lesser Caucasus, Azerbiadzhan SSR; in Russian). In *Voprosy Tafonomii i Paleobiologii*, Chaired by B. S. Soklov, pp. 39-44. SSSR, Akademiya Nauk, Vsesoyuznoe Paleontologicheskoe Obshchestvo. Trudy Sessi 20. Leningrad.
16. Aliyev, R. A.
    1978 Nakhozhdenie v Verkhnem Melu Yugo-Vostochnogo Kavkaza Pereotlozhennykh Okamenelostei (A Find of Index Fossils in Upper Cretaceous Deposits of the Southeastern Caucasus; in Russian). In *Voprosy Tafonomii i Paleobiologii*, Chaired by B. S. Soklov, pp. 44-48. SSSR, Akademiya Nauk, Vsesoyuznoe Paleontologicheskoe Obshchestvo. Trudy Sessi 20. Leningrad.
17. Allen, J., and J. B. M. Guy
    1984 Optimal Estimations of Individuals in Archaeological Faunal Assemblages: How Minimal Is the MNI? *Archaeology in Oceania* 19: 41-47.
18. Allen, J. R. L.
    1965 A Review of the Origin and Characteristics of Recent Alluvial Sediments. *Sedimentology* 5: 89-191.
19. Allen, J. R. L.
    1970 *Physical Processes of Sedimentation*. George Allen & Unwin, London.

20. Allen, J. R. L.
    1976 Bed Forms and Unsteady Processes: Some Concepts of Classification and Response Illustrated by Common One-Way Types. *Earth Surface Processes* 1: 361-374.
21. Ambrose, S. H.
    1986 Comment on Bunn and Kroll 1986. *Current Anthropology* 27: 443.
22. Anderson, C. M.
    1986 Predation and Primate Evolution. *Primates* 27: 15-39.
23. Anderson, J. L.
    1974 Osteophagia by Nyala and Two Related Accidents. *Lammergeyer* 21: 37-39.
24. Anderson, S., and C. A. Long
    1961 Small Mammals in Pellets of Barn Owls from Minaca, Chihuahua. *American Museum Novitates* 2052.
25. Andrews, P.
    1983 Small Mammal Diversity at Olduvai Gorge, Tanzania. In *Animals and Archaeology: 1. Hunters and Their Prey*, edited by J. Clutton-Brock and C. Grigson, pp. 77-85. British Archaeological Reports, BAR International Series No. 163. Oxford.
26. Andrews, P. and J. Cook
    1985 Natural Modification of Bones in a Temperate Setting. *Man* 20: 675-691.
27. Andrews, P., G. E. Meyer, D. R. Pilbeam, J. A. Van Couvering, and J. A. H. Van Couvering
    1981 The Miocene Fossil Beds of Maboko Island, Kenya: Geology, Age, Taphonomy and Paleontology. *Journal of Human Evolution* 10: 35-48.
28. Andrews, P., J. M. Lord, and E. M. Nesbit Evans
    1979 Patterns of Ecological Diversity in Fossil and Modern Mammalian Faunas. *Linnean Society of London. Biological Journal* 11: 177-205.
29. Anonymous
    1950 The Role of Earthworms and Insects in Soil Formation. *Soils and Fertilizers* 13: 157-160.
30. Antia, D. D. J.
    1979 Bone-Beds: A Review of Their Classification, Occurrence, Genesis, Diagenesis, Geochemistry, Paleoecology, Weathering, and Microbiotas. *Mercian Geology* 7: 93-174.
31. Appleby, R. M., and G. L. Jones
    1976 The Analogue Video Reshaper—A New Tool for Paleontologists. *Paleontology* 19: 565-586.
32. Archer, M.
    1974 Apparent Association of Bone and Charcoal of Different Origin and Age in Cave Deposits. *Queensland Museum, Brisbane. Memoirs* 17: 37-48.
33. Archer, M., I. M. Crawford, and D. Merrilees
    1980 Incisions, Breakages and Charring, Some Probably Man-Made, in Fossil Bones from Mammoth Cave, Western Australia. *Alcheringa* 4: 115-131.
34. Arens, W.
    1979 *The Man-eating Myth: Anthropology and Anthropophagy*. Oxford University Press, Oxford.
35. Arnold, A. J.
    1982 The Potential of Biometric Characters for Increased Stratigraphic Resolution in the Foraminiferal Record (Abstract). *Journal of Paleontology* 56(Supp. No. 2): 1.
36. Arnold, C. A.
    1941 The Petrifaction of Wood. *Mineralogist* 9: 323-324, 353-355.
37. Ascenzi, A., and G. Silvestrini
    1984 Bone-boring Marine Micro-organisms: An Experimental Investigation. *Journal of Human Evolution* 13: 531-536.
38. Atkinson, R. J. C.
    1957 Worms and Weathering. *Antiquity* 31: 219-233.
39. Avery, D. M.
    1984 Sampling Procedures and Cautionary Tales. In *Frontiers: Southern African Archaeology Today*, edited by M. Hall, G. Avery, D. M. Avery, M. L. Wilson, and A. J. B. Humphreys, pp. 375-379. British Archaeological Reports, BAR International Series No. 207. Oxford.
40. Avery, G.
    1984 Sacred Cows or Jackal Kitchens, Hyaena Middens and Bird Nests: Some Implications of Multiagent contributions to archaeological accumulations. In *Frontiers: Southern African Archaeology Today*, edited by M. Hall, G. Avery, D. M. Avery, M. L. Wilson, and A. J. B. Humphreys, pp. 344-348. British Archaeological Reports, BAR International Series No. 207. Oxford.
41. Avery, G.
    1984 Agencies and Numbers: The Faunal Workshop. In *Frontiers: Southern African Archaeology Today*, edited by M. Hall, G. Avery, D. M. Avery, M. L. Wilson, and A. J. B. Humphreys, pp. 329-333. British Archaeological Reports, BAR International Series No. 207. Oxford.
42. Bachinskii, G. A.
    1965 Principles of Taphonomic Classification in Relation to Discoveries of Terrestrial Vertebrates in Neogene and Anthropogene Deposits of the Ukraine. *Paleontologicheskii Sbornik* 1965: 65-72. (Translating Programme, RTS 7328, National Lending Library for Science and Technology, Boston Spa, Yorkshire).
43. Badgley, C. E.
    1982 *Community Reconstruction of a Siwulik Mammalian Assemblage*. Ph.D. dissertation, Yale University, New Haven. University Microfilms DA8310482, Ann Arbor.
44. Bagnold, R. A.
    1966 *An Approach to the Sediment Transport Problem from General Physics*. U. S. Geological Survey. Professional Paper 422-I.
45. Bagnold, R. A.
    1977 Bed Transport by Natural Rivers. *Water Resources Research* 13: 303-312.
46. Bailey, J. W., and J. K. Lundy
    n. d. Human Bone Sorting in an Artificial Fluviatile Environment: An Interpretive Method. Ms. on file with C. P. Koch.

47. Bailey, J. W., and J. K. Lundy
    1977 Hominid Taphonomy: Critical Transport Velocities of Human Skeletal Parts in an Aritifical Fluviatile Environment. Paper presented at the 30th annual Northwest Anthropological Conference, Victoria, British Columbia.
48. Baker, C. M.
    1978 The Size Effect: An Explanation of Variability in Surface Artifact Assemblage Content. *American Antiquity* 43: 288-293.
49. Baker, V. R.
    1974 Paleohydraulic Interpretation of Quaternary Alluvium Near Golden, Colorado. *Quaternary Research* 4: 94-112.
50. Baker, V. R., and D. F. Ritter
    1975 Competence of Rivers to Transport Coarse Bedload Material. *Geological Society of America. Bulletin* 86: 975-978.
51. Banks, E. E.
    1969 The Fragmentation Behavior of Thin-walled Metal Cylinders. *Journal of Applied Physics* 40: 437-438.
52. Baranov, V. N., A. N. Ivanov, and E. S. Muravin
    1978 K Volrosu o Tafonomii Verkhneyurskikh Ammonitov i Prichinakh Nedostatochnoi Izuchennosti Zhilykh Kamer (The Taphonomy of Upper Jurassic Ammonites and Some Unsatisfactory Studies of the Shells as Living Quarters; in Russian). In *Voprosy Tafonomii i Paleobiologii*, Chaired by B. S. Soklov, pp. 48-55. SSSR, Akademiya Nauk, Vsesoyuznoe Paleontologicheskoe Obshchestvo. Trudy Sessi 20. Leningrad.
53. Barash, D. P., P. Donovan, and R. Myrick
    1975 Clam Dropping Behavior of the Glaucous-winged Gull *(Larus glaucescens)*. *Wilson Bulletin* 87: 60-64.
54. Barbour, E. H.
    1931 The Giant Beaver, *Castoroides*, and the Common Beaver, *Castor*, in Nebraska. *Nebraska State Museum. Bulletin* 1: 171-186.
55. Barbour, E. P.
    1950 A Study of the Structure of Fresh and Fossil Human Bone by Means of the Electron Microscope. *American Journal of Physical Anthropology* 8: 315-329.
56. Barnosky, A. D.
    1985 Taphonomy and Herd Structure of the Extinct Irish Elk. *Science* 228: 340-344.
57. Bathurst, R. G. C.
    1964 Diagenesis and Paleoecology: A Survey. In *Approaches to Paleoecology*, edited by J. Imbrie and N. D. Newell, pp. 319-344. John Wiley, New York.
58. Bayer, U.
    1978 Finite Computations in Compaction Theory—Numerical Approximation or Physical Reality. *Neues Jahrbuch für Geologie und Paläontologie. Abhandlungen* 157: 176-185.
59. Baynes, A., D. Merrilees, and J. K. Porter
    1975 Mammal Remains from the Upper Levels of a Late Pleistocene Deposit in Western Australia. *Royal Society of Western Australia. Journal* 58: 97-126.
60. Bearder, S. K.
    1977 Feeding Habits of Spotted Hyaenas in a Woodland Habitat. *East African Wildlife Journal* 15: 263-280.
61. Beck, L. A.
    1985 Bivariate Analysis of Trace Elements in Bone. *Journal of Human Evolution* 14: 493-502.
62. Beebe, B. F.
    1983 Evidence of Carnivore Activity in a Late Pleistocene/Early Holocene Archaeological Site (Bluefish Cave I), Yukon Territory, Canada. In *Carnivores, Human Scavengers and Predators*, edited by G. M. LeMoine and A. S. MacEachern, pp. 1-14. (15th Annual Chacmool Conference, Proceedings). Archaeological Association, Department of Archaeology, University of Calgary, Alberta.
63. Beerbower, J. R., and D. Jordan
    1969 Application of Information Theory to Paleontologic Problems: Taxonomic Diversity. *Journal of Paleontology* 43: 1184-1198.
64. Begouen, C., and L. Begouen
    1937 Quelques Esquilles d'Os, du Magdalénien, Travaillées Comme de Silex. *Compte Rendue 12th Congrès Préhistorique de France*, pp. 685-688.
65. Behrensmeyer, A. K.
    1975 The Taphonomy and Paleoecology of Plio-Pleistocene Vertebrate Assemblages East of Lake Rudolf, Kenya. *Harvard University, Museum of Comparative Zoology. Bulletin* 146: 473-578.
66. Behrensmeyer, A. K.
    1975 Taphonomy and Paleoecology in the Hominid Fossil Record. *Yearbook of Physical Anthropology* 19: 36-50.
67. Behrensmeyer, A. K.
    1976 Fossil Assemblages in Relation to Sedimentary Environments in the East Rudolf Succession. In *Earliest Man and Environments in the Lake Rudolf Basin*, edited by Y. Coppens, F. C. Howell, G. L. Isaac, and R. E. F. Leakey, pp. 383-401. University of Chicago Press, Chicago.
68. Behrensmeyer, A. K.
    1978 Taphonomic and Ecologic Information from Bone Weathering. *Paleobiology* 4: 150-162.
69. Behrensmeyer, A. K.
    1978 The Habitat of Plio-Pleistocene Hominids in East Africa: Taphonomic and Micro-Stratigraphic Evidence. In *Early Hominids of Africa*, edited by C. J. Jolly, pp. 165-189. Duckworth, London.
70. Behrensmeyer, A. K.
    1981 Vertebrate Paleoecology in a Recent East African Ecosystem. In *Communities of the Past*, edited by J. Gray, A. J. Boucot, and W. B. N. Berry, pp. 591-615. Hutchinson Ross, Stroudsburg, Penna.
71. Behrensmeyer, A. K.
    1982 Time Resolution in Fluvial Vertebrate Assemblages. *Paleobiology* 8: 211-227.
72. Behrensmeyer, A. K.
    1982 Time Sampling Intervals in the Vertebrate Fossil Record. In *Proceedings of the 3rd North American Paleontological Convention*, 1: 41-45.

73. Behrensmeyer, A. K.
    1982 The Geological Context of Human Evolution. *Annual Review of Earth and Planetary Science* 10: 39-60.
74. Behrensmeyer, A. K.
    1984 Taphonomy and the Fossil Record. *American Scientist* 72: 558-566.
75. Behrensmeyer, A. K.
    1986 Comment on Binford and Stone 1986. *Current Anthropology* 27: 469.
76. Behrensmeyer, A. K.
    1986 Comment on Bunn and Kroll 1986. *Current Anthropology* 27: 443-444.
77. Behrensmeyer, A. K., and H. B. S. Cooke
    1985 Paleoenvironments, Stratigraphy, and Taphonomy in the African Pliocene and Early Pleistocene. In *Ancestors: The Hard Evidence*, edited by E. Delson, pp. 60-62. Alan R. Liss, New York.
78. Behrensmeyer, A. K., and D. E. Dechant
    1980 The Recent Bones of Amboseli Park, Kenya in Relation to East African Paleoecology. In *Fossils in the Making: Vertebrate Taphonomy and Paleoecology*, edited by A. K. Behrensmeyer and A. P. Hill, pp. 72-92. University of Chicago Press, Chicago.
79. Behrensmeyer, A. K., K. D. Gordon, and G. T. Yanagi.
    1986 Trampling as a Cause of Bone Surface Damage and Pseudo-cutmarks. *Nature* 319: 768-771.
80. Behrensmeyer, A. K., J. T. Gregory, and C. B. Hanson
    1974 Preliminary Report on Flume Experiments. Ms. on file with C. P. Koch.
81. Behrensmeyer, A. K., and S. M. Kidwell
    1985 Taphonomy's Contributions to Paleobiology. *Paleobiology* 11: 105-119.
82. Behrensmeyer, A. K., and D. E. Schindel
    1983 Resolving Time in Paleobiology. *Paleobiology* 9: 1-8.
83. Behrensmeyer, A. K., D. Western, and D. E. Dechant-Boaz
    1979 New Perspectives in Vertebrate Paleoecology from a Recent Bone Assemblage. *Paleobiology* 5: 12-21.
84. Beherensmeyer, A. K., G. T. Yanagi, and K. D. Gordon
    1989 Non-Human Modification in Miocene Fossils from Pakistan. In *Bone Modification*, edited by R. Bonnichsen and M. Sorg (1st International Bone Modification Conference, Proceedings). Center for the Study of the First Americans, Orono, Maine.
85. Bentzen, R.
    1962 The Powers-Yonkee Bison Trap. *Plains Anthropologist* 7: 113-118.
86. Berg, S.
    1963 The Determination of Bone Age. In *Methods of Forensic Science*, vol. 2, edited by F. Lundquist, pp. 231-252. Interscience, New York.
87. Berger, J.
    1983 Ecology and Catastrophic Mortality in Wild Horses: Implications for Interpreting Fossil Assemblages. *Science* 220: 1403-1404.
88. Berner, R. A.
    1969 Chemical Changes Affecting Dissolved Calcium During the Bacterial Decomposition of Fish and Clams in Sea Water. *Marine Geology* 7: 253-274.
89. Betancourt, J. L., and O. K. Davis
    1984 Packrat Middens from Canyon de Chelly, Northeastern Arizona: Paleoecological and Archaeological Implications. *Quaternary Research* 21: 56-64.
90. Biberson, P.
    1964 Torralba et Ambrona, Notes sur Deux Stations Acheuléenes d'Éléphants de la Vieille Castille. In *Miscelanea en Homenaje al Abate Henri Breuil, 1877-1961*, vol. 1, edited by E. Ripoll Perello, pp. 201-230. Instituto de Prehistoria y Arqueología, Barcelona.
91. Biberson, P., and E. Aguirre
    1965 Expériences de Taille d'Outils Prehistoriques dans des Os d'Éléphant. *Quaternaria* 7: 165-183.
92. Biddick, K. A., and J. Tomenchuck
    1975 Quantifying Continuous Lesions and Fractures on Long Bones. *Journal of Field Archaeology* 2: 239-249.
93. Binford, L. R.
    1963 An Analysis of Cremations from Three Michigan Sites. *Wisconsin Archaeologist* 44: 98-110.
94. Binford, L. R.
    1972 Analysis of a Cremated Burial from the Riverside Cemetery, Menominee County, Michigan. In *An Archaeological Perspective*, edited by L. R. Binford, pp. 383-389. (Studies in Archeology, edited by S. Struever) Seminar Press, New York.
95. Binford, L. R.
    1978 *Nunamiut Ethnoarchaeology*. Academic Press, New York.
96. Binford, L. R.
    1981 *Bones: Ancient Men and Modern Myths*. Academic Press, New York.
97. Binford, L. R.
    1982 Comment on White 1982. *Current Anthropology* 23: 177-181.
98. Binford, L. R.
    1983 Reply to Freeman 1983. *Current Anthropology* 24: 372-376.
99. Binford, L. R.
    1983 *In Pursuit of the Past*. Thames and Hudson, New York.
100. Binford, L. R.
    1984 Bones of Contention: A Reply to Glynn Isaac. (On G. Isaac's review of *Bones*, by L. R. Binford). *American Antiquity* 49: 164-167.
101. Binford, L. R.
    1984 *Faunal Remains from Klasies River Mouth*. Academic Press, New York.
102. Binford, L. R.
    1984 Butchery, Sharing and the Archaeological Record. *Journal of Anthropological Archaeology* 3: 235-237.
103. Binford, L. R.
    1985 Human Ancestors: Changing Views of Their Behavior. *Journal of Anthropological Archaeology* 4: 292-327.

104. Binford, L. R.
    1986 Comment on Bunn and Kroll 1986. *Current Anthropology* 27: 444-446.
105. Binford, L. R.
    1987 The Hunting Hypothesis, Archaeological Methods, and the Past. *Yearbook of Physical Anthropology* 30: 1-9.
106. Binford, L. R., and J. B. Bertram
    1977 Bone-Frequencies and Attritional Processes. In *For Theory Building in Archaeology*, edited by L. R. Binford, pp. 77-153. Academic Press, New York.
107. Binford, L. R., and C. K. Ho
    1985 Taphonomy at a Distance: Zhoukoudian, "The Cave Home of Beijing Man?" *Current Anthropology* 26: 413-442.
108. Binford, L. R., and L. S. Mick
    1983 Review of *Bison Kills and Bone Counts*, by J. D. Speth. *Zooarchaeological Research News* 2(4): 10-12.
109. Binford, L. R., and N. M. Stone
    1986 Zoukoudian: A Closer Look. *Current Anthropology* 27: 453-475.
110. Binford, L. R., and N. M. Stone
    1987 On Zhoukoudian Reply to Comments (on Binford and Stone 1986). *Current Anthropology* 28: 102-105.
111. Binford, L. R., and N. M. Stone
    1987 On Inferences from the Zhoukoudian Fauna: Reply to Bunn and Kroll 1987 (Comments on Binford and Stone 1986). *Current Anthropology* 28: 358-362.
112. Binford, L. R., and L. C. Todd
    1982 On Arguments for the "Butchering" of Giant Geladas. (Comments on Shipman, Bosler, and Davis 1981). *Current Anthropology* 23: 108-110.
113. Bird, F., H. Becker, J. Healer, and M. Messer
    1968 Experimental Determination of the Mechanical Properties of Bone. *Aerospace Medicine* 39: 44-48.
114. Bird, R. D.
    1961 *Ecology of the Aspen Parkland of Western Canada in Relation to Land Use*. Canada. Department of Agriculture. Research Branch, Ottawa. Publication No. 1066.
115. Bishop, W. W.
    1980 Paleogeomorphology and Continental Taphonomy. In *Fossils in the Making: Vertebrate Taphonomy and Paleoecology*, edited by A. K. Behrensmeyer and A. P. Hill, pp. 20-37. University of Chicago Press, Chicago.
116. Black, D. (editor)
    1933 *Fossil Man in China*. Geological Survey of China. Memoirs, Series A, No. 11.
117. Blatt, H., G. V. Middleton, and R. Murray
    1972 *Origin of Sedimentary Rocks*. Prentice-Hall, Englewood Cliffs, New Jersey
118. Blumenschine, R. J.
    1986 *Early Hominid Scavenging Opportunities Implications of Carcass Availability in the Serengeti and Ngorongoro Ecosystems*. British Archaeological Reports, BAR International Series No. 283, Oxford.
119. Blumenschine, R. J.
    1986 Carcass Consumption Sequences and the Archaeological Distinction of Scavenging and Hunting. *Journal of Human Evolution* 15: 639-659.
120. Blumenschine, R. J.
    1986 Comment on Bunn and Kroll 1986. *Current Anthropology* 27: 446.
121. Blumenschine, R. J., and T. M. Caro
    1986 Unit Flesh Weights of Some East African Bovids. *African Journal of Ecology* 24: 273-286.
122. Blumenschine, R. J.
    1987 Characteristics of an Early Hominid Scavenging Niche. *Current Anthropology* 28: 383-407.
123. Boaz, N. T., and J. Hampel
    1978 Strontium Content of Fossil Tooth Enamel and Diet of Early Hominids. *Journal of Paleontology* 52: 928-933.
124. Boaz, N. T., and A. K. Behrensmeyer
    1976 Preliminary Investigation into Transport of Hominid Bones in Fluviatile Environments. *American Journal of Physical Anthropology* 45: 53-60.
125. Boeck, B.
    1986 Rodent Ecology and Burrowing Behavior: Predicted Effects on Archaeological Site Formation. *American Antiquity* 51: 589-603.
126. Bokonyi, S.
    1970 A New Method for the Determination of the Number of Individuals in Animal Bone Material. *American Journal of Anthropology* 74: 291-292.
127. Bonfield, W.
    1975 Deformation and Fracture Characteristics of the Cooperton Mammoth Bones. *Great Plains Journal* 14: 158-164.
128. Bonfield, W., and C. H. Li
    1965 Deformation and Fracture of Ivory. *Journal of Applied Physics* 36: 3181-3184.
129. Bonfield, W., and C. H. Li
    1966 Deformation and Fracture of Bone. *Journal of Applied Physics* 37: 869-875.
130. Bonnichsen, R.
    1973 Some Operational Aspects of Human and Animal Bone Alteration. In *Mammalian Osteo-Archaeology: North America*, by B. Miles Gilbert, pp. 9-24. Missouri Archaeological Society. Special Publications. Columbia.
131. Bonnichsen, R.
    1975 On Faunal Analysis and the Australopithecines. (Reply to Read-Martin and Read 1975). *Current Anthropology* 16: 635.
132. Bonnichsen, R.
    1975 Bone Flaking Techniques Applied to Mid-Wisconsin Fauna from the Old Crow Basin, Yukon Territory. Paper presented at the 13th Pacific Science Congress, Vancouver.
133. Bonnichsen, R.
    1978 Critical Arguments for Pleistocene Artifacts from the Old Crow Basin, Yukon: A Preliminary Statement. In *Early Man in America*, edited by A. L. Bryan, pp. 102-118. Occasional Papers No. 1. Department of Anthropology, University of Alberta, Edmonton.

134. Bonnichsen, R.
   1979 *Pleistocene Bone Technology in the Beringian Refugium*. Archaeological Survey of Canada, Paper No. 89. Mercury Series. National Museum of Man, Ottawa.
135. Bonnichsen, R.
   1982 Bone Technology as a Taphonomic Factor: An Introductory Statement. *Canadian Journal of Anthropology* 2: 137-144.
136. Bonnichsen, R.
   1983 The Broken Bone Controversy: Some Issues Important for the Study of Early Archaeological Sites. In *Carnivores, Human Scavengers and Predators*, edited by G. M. LeMoine and A. S. MacEachern, pp. 271-284. (15th Annual Chacmool Conference, Proceedings). Archaeological Association, Department of Archaeology, University of Calgary, Alberta.
137. Bonnichsen, R.
   1983 Review of *Bones*, by L. R. Binford. *Plains Anthropologist* 28: 247-249.
138. Bonnichsen, R.
   1989 An Introduction to Taphonomy with an Archaeological Focus. In *Bone Modification*, edited by R. Bonnichsen and M. Sorg (1st International Bone Modification Conference, Proceedings). Center for the Study of the First Americans, Orono, Maine.
139. Manuscript deleted from bibliography.
140. Bonnichsen, R.
   1989 Construction of Taphonomic Models: Theory, Assumptions, Procedures. In *Bone Modification*, edited by R. Bonnichsen and M. Sorg (1st International Bone Modification Conference, Proceedings). Center for the Study of the First Americans, Orono, Maine.
141. Bonnichsen, R., and D. Sanger
   1977 Integrating Faunal Analysis. *Canadian Journal of Archaeology* 1: 109-133.
142. Bonnichsen, R., and R. T. Will
   1980 Cultural Modification of Bone. In *Mammalian Osteology*, edited by B. Miles Gilbert, pp. 7-30. B. M. Gilbert, Laramie, Wyoming.
143. Bonucci, E., and G. Graziani
   1975 Comparative Thermogravimetric X-ray Difraction and Electron Microscope Investigations of Burnt Bones of Recent, Ancient and Prehistoric Age. *Atti' Della Accademia Nazionale dei Lincei Scientifico Fisico Matem. Natur. Series No. 8.* 59: 517-534.
144. Bornemissza, G. F.
   1957 An Analysis of Arthropod Succession in Carrion and the Effects of its Decomposition on the Soil Fauna. *Australian Journal of Zoology* 5: 1-12.
145. Borrero, L. A.
   1985 Comment on Binford and Ho 1985 (Reply by Binford and Ho). *Current Anthropology* 26: 431.
146. Boucot, A. J.
   1953 Life and Death Assemblages Among Fossils. *American Journal of Science* 251: 25-40.
147. Boucot, A. J., W. Brace, and R. DeMar
   1958 Distribution of Brachiopod and Pelecypod Shells by Currents. *Journal of Sedimentary Petrology* 28: 321-332.
148. Bown, T. M., and M. J. Kraus
   1981 Lower Eocene Alluvial Paleosols (Willwood Formation, Northwest Wyoming, USA) and Their Significance for Paleoecology, Paleoclimatology, and Basin Analysis. *Palaeogeography, Palaeoclimatology, Palaeoecology* 34: 1-30.
149. Bown, T. M., and M. J. Kraus
   1981 Vertebrate Fossil-Bearing Paleosol Units (Willwood Formation, Lower Eocene, Northwest Wyoming, USA): Implications for Taphonomy, Biostratigraphy, and Assemblage Analysis. *Palaeogeography, Palaeoclimatology, Palaeoecology* 34: 31-56.
150. Boyd, D. W., and N. D. Newell
   1972 Taphonomy and Diagenesis of a Permian Fossil Assemblage from Wyoming. *Wyoming Journal of Paleontology* 46: 1-14.
151. Boyer, P.
   1958 Influence des Remaniements par le Termite et de l'Érosion sur l'Évolution Pédogénétique de la Termitière Épigée de *Bellicositermes Rex*. Académie des Sciences, Compte Rendus Hebdomadaires des Séances, Paris. 247: 749-751. Paris.
152. Brain, C. K.
   1967 Bone Weathering and the Problem of Bone Pseudo-Tools. *South African Journal of Science* 63: 97-99.
153. Brain, C. K.
   1967 Hottentot Food Remains and Their Bearing on the Interpretation of Fossil Bone Assemblages. *Namib Desert Research Station. Scientific Paper* 32: 1-11.
154. Brain, C. K.
   1969 The Contribution of the Namib Desert Hottentots to an Understanding of Australopithecine. *Namib Desert Research Station. Scientific Paper* 39: 13-22.
155. Brain, C. K.
   1969 Faunal Remains from the Bushman Rock Shelter, Eastern Transvaal. *South African Archaeological Bulletin* 24: 52-55.
156. Brain, C. K.
   1969 The Probable Role of Leopards as Predators of the Swartkrans Australopithecines. *South African Archaeological Bulletin* 24: 170-171.
157. Brain, C. K.
   1970 New Finds at Swartkrans Australopithecus Site. *Nature* 225: 112-119.
158. Brain, C. K.
   1972 An Attempt to Reconstruct the Behaviour of Australopithecines: The Evidence for Interpersonal Violence. *Zoologica Africana* 7: 379-401.

159. Brain, C. K.
    1974 Some Suggested Procedures in the Analysis of Bone Accumulations from Southern African Quaternary Sites. *Transvaal Museum, Pretoria. Annals* 29: 1-8.
160. Brain, C. K.
    1975 An Interpretation of the Bone Assemblage from the Kromdraai Australopithecine Site, South Africa. In *Paleoanthropology: Morphology and Paleoecology*, edited by R. H. Tuttle, pp. 225-243. Mouton, The Hague.
161. Brain, C. K.
    1975 An Introduction to the South African Australopithecine Bone Accumulations. In *Archaeozoological Studies*, edited by A. T. Clason, pp. 109-119. American Elsevier, New York.
162. Brain, C. K.
    1976 Some Principles in the Interpretation of Bone Accumulations Associated with Man. In *Human Origins*, edited by G. L. Isaac and E. McCown, pp. 97-116. W. A. Benjamin, Menlo Park, California.
163. Brain, C. K.
    1978 Some Aspects of the South African Australopithecine Sites and Their Bone Accumulations. In *Early Hominids of Africa*, edited by C. J. Jolly, pp. 131-161. St. Martin's Press, New York.
164. Brain, C. K.
    1980 Some Criteria for the Recognition of Bone Collecting Agencies in African Caves. In *Fossils in the Making: Vertebrate Taphonomy and Paleoecology*, edited by A. K. Behrensmeyer and A. P. Hill, pp. 107-130. University of Chicago Press, Chicago.
165. Brain, C. K.
    1980 Swartkrans as a Case Study in African Cave Taphonomy (Summary). *Palaeontologia Africana* 23: 73-74.
166. Brain, C. K.
    1981 *The Hunters or the Hunted? An Introduction to African Cave Taphonomy*. University of Chicago Press, Chicago.
167. Brain, C. K.
    1985 Interpreting Early Hominid Death Assemblages: The Rise of Taphonomy Since 1925. In *Hominid Evolution Past, Present and Future*, edited by P. V. Tobias, pp. 41-46. Alan R. Liss, New York.
168. Brain, C. K.
    1985 Cultural and Taphonomic Comparisons of Hominids from Swartkrans and Sterkfontein. In *Ancestors: The Hard Evidence*, edited by E. Delson pp. 72-75. Alan R. Liss, New York.
169. Brain, C. K.
    1989 The Evidence for Bone Modification by Early Hominids in Southern Africa. In *Bone Modification*, edited by R. Bonnichsen and M. Sorg (1st International Bone Modification Conference, Proceedings). Center for the Study of the First Americans, Orono, Maine.
170. Brain, C. K., and G. Turner
    1984 Problems in Unravelling Multi-agent Involvement in Bone Accumulations. In *Frontiers: Southern African Archaeology Today*, edited by M. Hall, G. Avery, D. M. Avery, M. L. Wilson, and A. J. B. Humphreys, pp. 340-343. British Archaeological Reports, BAR International Series No. 207. Oxford.
171. Breder, C. M.
    1957 A Note on Preliminary States in the Fossilization of Fishes. *Copeia* 2: 132-135.
172. Brenchley, P. J., and G. Newall
    1970 Flume Experiments on the Orientation and Transport of Models and Shell Valves. *Palaeogeography, Palaeoclimatology, Palaeoecology* 7: 185-220.
173. Breuil, H. A.
    1932 Le Feu et l'Industrie de Pierre et d'Os dans le Gisement du "Sinanthropus" a Chou Kou Tien. *Anthropologie* 42: 1-17.
174. Breuil, H. A.
    1934 De l'Importance de la Solifluxion dans l'Etude des Terrains Quaternaires du Nord de la France et des Pays Voisins. *Revue de Geographie Physique et de Geologie Dynamique* 8: 269-338.
175. Breuil, H. A.
    1938 The Use of Bone Implements in the Old Paleolithic Period. *Antiquity* 12: 56-67.
176. Breuil, H. A.
    1939 *Bone and Antler Industry of the Choukoutien Sinanthropus Site*. Palaeontologia Sinica, Series D, New Series No. 6 (Whole Series No. 117), Geological Survey of China, Peiking.
177. Breuil, H. A., and L. Barral
    1955 Bois de Cervides et Autres os Travaillés Sommairement au Paléolithique Ancien du Vieux Monde et au Moustérien des Grottes de Grimaldi et de l'Observations de Monaco. Monaco. *Musée d'Anthropologie Préhistorique. Bulletin* 2: 3-26.
178. Breuil, H. A., and R. Lantier
    1959 *The Men of the Old Stone Age*. St. Martin's Press, New York.
179. Bridge, J. S.
    1977 Flow, Bed Topography, Grain Size, and Sedimentary Structure in Open Channel Beds: A Three-Dimensional Model. *Earth Surface Processes* 2: 401-416.
180. Brink, J.
    1984 Reivew of R. G. Klein, and K. Cruz-Uribe, *The Analysis of Animal Bones from Archaeological Sites*. *Zooarchaeological Research News* 3(4): 11-13.
181. Brink, J. S.
    1987 *The Archaeozoology of Florisbad, Orange Free State*. Nasionale Museum, Bloemfontein. Memoirs No. 24.
182. Bromage, T. G.
    1984 Interpretation of Scanning Electron Microscopic Images of Abraded Forming Bone Surfaces. *American Journal of Physical Anthropology* 64: 161-178.

183. Bromage, T. G., and A. Boyde
    1984 Microscopic Criteria for the Determination of Directionality of Cutmarks on Bone. *American Journal of Physical Anthropology* 65: 359-366.
184. Bromley, R. G.
    1970 Borings as Trace Fossils and *Entobia cretecea* (Portlock), as an Example. In *Trace Fossils*, edited by T. P. Crimes and J. C. Harper, pp. 49-90. Seel House Press, Liverpool.
185. Brongersma-Sanders, M.
    1957 Mass Mortality in the Sea. *Geological Society of America. Memoirs* 67: 941-1010.
186. Brooks, R. H.
    1967 A Comparative Analysis of Bone from Locality 2 (C1-245) Tule Springs, Nevada. *Nevada State Museum, Carson City. Anthropological Papers* 13: 402-411.
187. Brothwell, D. R.
    1961 Cannibalism in Early Britain. *Antiquity* 35: 304-307.
188. Brothwell, D. R.
    1976 Further Evidence of Bone Chewing by Ungulates: The Sheep of North Ronaldsay, Orkney. *Journal of Archaeological Science* 3: 179-182.
189. Brown, A. B., and R. L. Blakely
    1985 Biocultural Adaptation as Reflected in Trace Element Distribution. *Journal of Human Evolution* 14: 461-468.
190. Brown, P., and D. Tuzin
    1983 *The Ethnography of Canaibalism.* Society for Psychological Anthropology, Washington.
191. Brumley, J. H.
    1973 Quantitative Methods in the Analysis of Butchered Faunal Remains: A Suggested Approach. *Archaeology in Montana* 14: 1-40.
192. Bryan, A. L.
    1983 Bone Alteration Patterns as Clues for the Identification of Early Man Sites or, an Attempt to Demythify the Search for Early Americans. In *Carnivores, Human Scavengers and Predators*, edited by G. M. LeMoine and A. S. MacEachern, pp. 193-217. (15th Annual Chacmool Conference, Proceedings). Archaeological Association, Department of Archaeology, University of Calgary, Alberta.
193. Bryan, A. L., J. M. Cruxent, R. Gruhn, and C. Ochsenius
    1978 An El Jobo Mastodon Kill at Taima-Taima, Venezuela. *Science* 200: 1275-1277.
194. Buckland, W.
    1823 *Reliquiae Diluvianae.* John Murray, London.
195. Buczko, C. M., and L. Vas
    1977 Effects of Climate on the Chemical Composition of Fossil Bones. *Nature* 269: 792-793.
196. Buikstra, J. E., and M. Swegle
    1989 Bone Modification Due to Burning: Experimental Evidence. In *Bone Modification*, edited by R. Bonnichsen and M. Sorg (1st International Bone Modification Conference, Proceedings). Center for the Study of the First Americans, Orono, Maine.
197. Bunn, H. T.
    1981 Archaeological Evidence for Meat-eating by Plio-Pleistocene Hominids from Koobi Fora and Olduvai Gorge. *Nature* 291: 574-577.
198. Bunn, H. T.
    1982 Animal Bones and Archaeological Inference. (Review of *Bones*, by L. R. Binford). *Science* 215: 494-495.
199. Bunn, H. T.
    1982 *Meat Eating and Human Evolution: Studies on the Diet and Subsistence Patterns of Plio-Pleistocene Hominids in East Africa.* Ph. D. dissertation, University of California, Berkeley. University Microfilms DA8312768, Ann Arbor.
200. Bunn, H. T.
    1983 Comparative Analysis of Modern Bone Assemblages from a San Hunter-Gatherer Camp in the Kalahari Desert, Botswana, and from a Spotted Hyena Den Near Nairobi, Kenya. In *Animals and Archaeology: 1. Hunters and Their Prey*, edited by J. Clutton-Brock and C. Grigson, pp. 143-148. British Archaeological Reports, BAR International Series No. 163. Oxford.
201. Bunn, H. T.
    1983 Evidence of the Diet and Subsistence Patterns of Plio-Pleistocene Hominids at Koobi Fora, Kenya, and at Olduvai Gorge, Tanzania. In *Animals and Archaeology: 1. Hunters and Their Prey*, edited by J. Clutton-Brock and C. Grigson, pp. 21-30. British Archaeological Reports, BAR International Series No. 163. Oxford.
202. Bunn, H. T.
    1986 Patterns of Skeletal Representation and Hominid Subsistence Activities at Olduvai Gorge, Tanzania, and Koobi Fora, Kenya. *Journal of Human Evolution* 15: 673-690.
203. Bunn, H. T.
    1987 Comment on Blumenschine 1987, with reply. *Current Anthropology* 28: 394-396.
204. Bunn, H. T.
    1989 Diagnosing Plio-Pleistocene Hominid Activity with Bone Fracture Evidence. In *Bone Modification*, edited by R. Bonnichsen and M. Sorg (1st International Bone Modification Conference, Proceedings). Center for the Study of the First Americans, Unverstiy of Maine, Orono.
205. Bunn, H. T., and R. J. Blumenschine
    1987 On "Theoretical Framework and Tests" of Early Hominid Meat and Marrow Acquisition: A Reply to Shipman (Comment on Shipman 1986). *American Anthropologist* 89: 444-448.
206. Bunn, H. T., K. J. W. K. Harris, G. L. Isaac, Z. Kaufulu, E. Kroll, K. D. Schick, N. Toth, and A. K. Behrensmeyer
    1980 FxJj50, an Early Pleistocene Site in Northern Kenya. *World Archaeology* 12: 109-136.
207. Bunn, H. T., and E. M. Kroll
    1986 Systematic butchery by Plio/Pleistocene hominids at Olduvai Gorge, Tanzania. *Current Anthropology* 27: 431-452.

208. Bunn, H. T., and E. M. Kroll
   1987 On Inferences from the Zhoukoudian Fauna (Comment on Binford and Stone 1986). *Current Anthropology* 28: 199-202.
209. Buntley, G. J., and R. I. Papendick
   1960 Worm-Worked Soils of Eastern South Dakota, Their Morphology and Classification. *Soil Science Society. Proceedings* 24: 128-132.
210. Burnstein, A. H., J. D. Currey, V. H. Frankel, and D. T. Reilly
   1972 The Ultimate Properties of Bone Tissue: The Effects of Yielding. *Journal of Biomechanics* 5: 35-44.
211. Burt, T. P., and P. J. Williams
   1976 Hydraulic Conductivity in Frozen Soils. *Earth Surface Processes* 1: 349-360.
212. Buskirk, S. W., and S. O. MacDonald
   1984 Seasonal Food Habits of Marten in South-central Alaska. *Canadian Journal of Zoology* 62: 944-950.
213. Butler, P. R.
   1977 Movement of Cobbles in a Gravelbed Stream During a Flood Season. *Geological Society of America. Memoirs* 88: 1072-1074.
214. Cadee, G. C.
   1968 *Molluscan Biocoenoses and Thanatocoenoses in the Ria de Arosa, Galicia, Spain*. E. J. Brill, Leiden.
215. Cahen, D., and J. Moeyersons
   1977 Subsurface Movements of Stone Artefacts and Their Implications for the Prehistory of Central Africa. *Nature* 266: 812-815.
216. Camp, C. L., and H. J. Allison
   1961 *Bibliography of Fossil Vertebrates, 1949-1953*. Geological Society of America. Memoirs 84.
217. Camp, C. L., H. J. Allison, R. H. Nichols, and H. McGinnis
   1968 *Bibliography of Fossil Vertebrates, 1959-1963*. Geological Society of America. Memoirs 117.
218. Camp, C. L., H. J. Allison, and R. H. Nichols
   1964 *Bibliography of Fossil Vertebrates, 1954-1958*. Geological Society of America. Memoirs 92.
219. Camp, C. L., R. H. Nichols, B. Brajnikov, C. Fulton, and J. A. Bacskai
   1972 *Bibliography of Fossil Vertebrates, 1964-1968*. Geological Society of America. Memoirs 134.
220. Camp, C. L., D. N. Taylor, and S. P. Welles
   1942 *Bibliography of Fossil Vertebrates, 1934-1938*. Geological Society of America. Special Paper 42.
221. Camp, C. L., and V. L. VanderHoof
   1940 *Bibliography of Fossil Vertebrates, 1928-1933*. Geological Society of America. Special Paper 27.
222. Camp, C. L., S. P. Welles, and M. Green
   1949 *Bibliography of Fossil Vertebrates, 1939-1943*. Geological Society of America. Memoirs 37.
223. Camp, C. L., S. P. Welles, and M. Green
   1953 *Bibliography of Fossil Vertebrates, 1944-1948*. Geological Society of America. Memoirs 57.
224. Campbell, J. B., and C. G. Sampson
   1971 *A New Analysis of Kent's Cavern, Devonshire, England*. University of Oregon, Eugene. Department of Anthropology. Anthropological Papers No. 3.
225. Camps-Fabrer, H. (editor)
   1974 *Colloque International sur l'Industrie de l'Os dans la Prehistoire*, 1st (Abbaye de Senanque, Gordes, France, 1974). Editions de l'Universite de Provence, Aix-en-Provence.
226. Canby, T. Y.
   1979 The Search for the First Americans. *National Geographic Magazine* 156: 330-363.
227. Carnot, A.
   1893 Recherches sur la Composition Générale et la Teneur en Fluor des Os Modernes et des Os Fossiles des Différents Ages. *Annales des Mines* 3: 155-195.
228. Carver, R. E. (editor)
   1971 *Procedures in Sedimentary Petrology*. Wiley-Interscience, New York.
229. Case, E. C.
   1935 Description of a Collection of Associated Skeletons of *Trimerorhachis*. University of Michigan, Ann Arbor. Museum of Paleontology. Contributions 4: 227-274.
230. Casteel, R. W.
   1971 Differential Bone Destruction: Some Comments. *American Antiquity* 36: 466-469.
231. Casteel, R. W.
   1972 Some Biases in the Recovery of Archaeological Faunal Remains. *Prehistoric Society. Proceedings* 38: 382-388.
232. Casteel, R. W.
   1975 Estimation of Size, Minimum Numbers of Individuals, and Seasonal Dating by Means of Fish Scales from Archaeological Sites. In *Archaeozoological Studies*, edited by A. T. Clason, pp. 70-86.
233. Casteel, R. W.
   1977 Characterization of Faunal Assemblages and the Minimum Number of Individuals Determined from Paired Elements: Continuing Problems in Archaeology. *Journal of Archaeological Science* 4: 125-134.
234. Casteel, R. W.
   1978 Faunal Assemblages and the "Wiegemethode" or Weight Method. *Journal of Field Archaeology* 5: 71-77.
235. Casteel, R. W., and D. K. Grayson
   1977 Terminological Problems in Quantitative Faunal Analysis. *World Archaeology* 9: 235-242.
236. Caughley, G.
   1966 Mortality Patterns in Mammals. *Ecology* 47: 906-918.
237. Chaplin, R. E.
   1971 *The Study of Animal Bones from Archaeological Sites*. Seminar Press, London.
238. Chapman, R. F., and J. H. P. Sankey
   1955 The Larger Invertebrate Fauna of Three Rabbit Carcasses. *Journal of Animal Ecology* 24: 395-402.
239. Chave, K. E.
   1960 Carbonate Skeletons to Limestones: Problems. *New York Academy of Sciences. Transactions* Series 2, 23: 14-24.
240. Chave, K. E.
   1964 Skeletal Durability and Preservation. In *Approaches to Paleoecology*, edited by J. Imbrie and N. D. Newell, pp. 377-387. John Wiley, New York.

241. Chave, K. E., K. S. Deffeyes, P. K. Weyl, R. M. Garrels, and M. E. Thompson
　　1962　Observations on the Solubility of Skeletal Carbonates in Aqueous Solutions. *Science* 137: 33-34.
242. Cheng, T.-K., and C. Tang
　　1985　Comment on Binford and Ho 1985 (Reply by Binford and Ho). *Current Anthropology* 26: 431.
243. Chenoweth, P. A.
　　1952　Statistical Methods Applied to Trentonian Stratigraphy in New York. *Geological Society of America. Bulletin* 63: 521-560.
244. Chisholm, B. S., D. E. Nelson, K. A. Hobson, H. P. Schwarcz, and M. Knyp
　　1983　Carbon Isotope Measurement Techniques for Bone Collagen: Notes for the Archaeologist. *Journal of Archaeological Science* 10: 355-360.
245. Clark, J., and K. K. Kietzke
　　1967　Oligocene Sedimentation, Stratigraphy, Paleoecology, and Paleoclimatology in the Big Badlands of South Dakota, edited by J. Clark, J. R. Beerbower, and K. K. Kietzk, pp. 111-129. Fieldiana. Geology Memoirs No. 5.
246. Clark, J. D.
　　1972　Palaeolithic Butchery Practices. In *Man, Settlement and Urbanism*, edited by P. T. Ucko, R. Tringham, and G. W. Dimbleby, pp. 146-156. Duckworth, London.
247. Clark, W. E. L.
　　1957　Humans and Hominids. (Review of *The Osteodontokeratic Culture of Australopithecus Prometheus*, by R. A. Dart.) *Nature* 180: 156.
248. Clarke, R. J.
　　1966　Introductory Notes on the Use and Habitation of Caves by Man South of the Sahara. *Cave Exploration Group of East Africa. Bulletin* 1: 70-114.
249. Clason, A. T., and W. Prummel
　　1977　Collecting, Sieving and Archaeozoological Research. *Journal of Archaeological Science* 4: 171-175.
250. Clifton, H. E., and S. Boggs, Jr.
　　1970　Concave-up Pelecypod *(Psephidia)* Shells in Shallow Marine Sand, Elk River Beds, Southwestern Oregon. *Journal of Sedimentary Petrology* 40: 888-897.
251. Clutton-Brock, J.
　　1975　A System for the Retrieval of Data Relating to Animal Remains from Archaeological Sites. In *Archaeozoological Studies*, edited by A. T. Clason, p. 21-34. American Elsevier, New York.
252. Coe, M.
　　1978　The Decomposition of Elephant Carcasses in the Tsavo (East) National Park, Kenya. *Journal of Arid Environments* 1: 71-86.
253. Coe, M.
　　1980　The Role of Modern Ecological Studies in the Reconstruction of Paleoenvironments in Sub-Saharan Africa. In *Fossils in the Making: Vertebrate Taphonomy and Paleoecology*, edited by A. Behrensmeyer and A. P. Hill, pp. 55-67. University of Chicago Press, Chicago.
254. Cole, G. H.
　　1961　*Culture Change in the Middle-Upper Pleistocene Transition in Africa*. Unpublished Ph. D. dissertation, University of Chicago, Chicago.
255. Cole, G. H.
　　1967　The Later Acheulian and Sangoan of Southern Uganda. In *Background to Evolution in Africa*, edited by W. W. Bishop and J. D. Clark, pp. 481-528. University of Chicago Press, Chicago.
256. Cole, J. E.
　　1954　Buffalo *(Bison bison)* killed by fire. *Journal of Mammalogy* 35: 453-454.
257. Cones, H. R.
　　1968　Selectivity in Fossil Preservation as Shown by a Comparison of Fossil and Modern Barnacle Populations. *Chesapeake Science* 9: 61-63.
258. Conkey, M. W.
　　1981　What Can We Do with Broken Bones? *New York Academy of Sciences. Annals* 376: 35-52.
259. Converse, H. H.
　　1989　A Rapid Mold Making Technique Using Silicone Rubber. In *Bone Modification*, edited by R. Bonnichsen and M. Sorg (1st International Bone Modification Conference, Proceedings). Center for the Study of the First Americans, Orono, Maine.
260. Conybeare, A., and G. A. Haynes
　　1984　Observations on Elephant Mortality and Bones in Water Holes. *Quaternary Research* 22: 189-200.
261. Cook, J.
　　1986　The Application of Scanning Electron Microscopy to Taphonomic and Archaeological Problems. In *Studies in the Palaeolithic of Britain and Northwest Europe*, edited by D. A. Roe, pp. 143-163. British Archaeological Reports, BAR International Series No. 296. Oxford.
262. Cook, J.
　　1986　Marked Human Bones from Gough's Cave, Somerset. *University of Bristol Spelaeology Society. Proceedings* 17: 275-285.
263. Cook, S. F.
　　1951　The Fossilization of Human Bone: Calcium, Phosphate, and Carbonate. *University of California Publications in American Archaeology and Ethnology* 40: 263-280.
264. Cook, S. F., and R. F. Heizer
　　1952　*The Fossilization of Bone: Organic Components and Water*. University of California, Berkeley. Department of Anthropology, California Archaeological Survey. Report No. 17.
265. Cook, S. F., S. T. Brooks, and H. Ezra-Cohn
　　1961　The Process of Fossilization. *Southwestern Journal of Anthropology* 17: 355-364.
266. Corfield, T. F.
　　1973　Elephant Mortality in Tsavo National Park, Kenya. *East African Wildlife Journal* 11: 339-368.
267. Cornaby, B. W.
　　1974　Carrion Reduction by Animals in Contrasting Tropical Habitats. *Biotropica* 6: 51-63.
268. Cornwall, I. W.
　　1974　*Bones for the Archaeologist*. J. M. Dent, London.

269. Corte, A. E.
    1963 Particle Sorting by Repeated Freezing and Thawing. *Science* 142: 499-501.
270. Coryndon, S. C.
    1964 Bone Remains in the Caves. In The Lava Caves of Mt. Suswa, Kenya, edited by P. E. Glover, E. C. Glover, T. E. Trump, and L. E. D. Waterridge. *Studies in Speleology* 1: 60.
271. Crader, D. C.
    1974 *The Effects of Scavengers on Bone Material from a Large Mammal: An Experiment Conducted Among the Bisa of the Luangwa Valley, Zambia*. Archaeological Survey Monograph 4. University of California, Los Angeles. Institute of Archaeology.
272. Crader, D. C.
    1981 *Hunters Alongside Farmers: Faunal Remains from Chencherere II Rockshelter, Malawi*. Ph.D. dissertation, University of California, Berkeley, University Microfilms 8200063, Ann Arbor.
273. Crader, D. C.
    1984 Faunal Remains from Chencherere II Rock Shelter, Malawi. *South African Archaeological Bulletin* 39: 37-52.
274. Crader, D. C.
    1984 *Hunters in Iron Age Malawi: The Zooarchaeology of Chencherere Rockshelter*. Malawi. Department of Antiquities. Publication No. 21.
275. Crick, R. E.
    1978 A Probabilist and Multivariate Method of Paleobiogeographic Analysis: An Alternative Approach. Paper presented at the 13th Annual Meeting, Northeastern Section of the Geological Society of America, Boston.
276. Cruz-Uribe, K., and R. G. Klein
    1986 Pascal Programs for Computing Taxonomic Abundance in Samples of Fossil Mammals. *Journal of Archaeological Science* 13: 171-187.
277. Cuffey, R. J., and D. E. Hattin
    1965 Kansas Chalk Gnawed by Desert Cottontail. *Journal of Mammalogy* 46: 696-697.
278. Currey, J. D.
    1964 Three Analogies to Explain the Mechanical Properties of Bone. *Biorheology* 2: 1-10.
279. Curtis, J. D., and E. L. Kozicky
    1944 Observations on the Eastern Porcupine. *Journal of Mammalogy* 25: 137-146.
280. D'Andrea, C. A., and R. M. Gotthardt
    1984 Predator and Scavenger Modification of Recent Equid Skeletal Assemblages. *Arctic* 37: 276-283.
281. Dailey, R. C.
    1982 Time of Death. Program of the 34th Annual Meeting of the American Academy of Forensic Sciences, p. 98. Colorado Springs, Colorado.
282. Dallman, J. E.
    1984 Book Review of *Taphonomy and Paleoecology of the Christensen Bog Mastodon Bone Bed*. (By R. W. Graham, J. A. Holman, and P. W. Parmalee). *Wisconsin Archaeologist* 65: 181-182.
283. Damuth, J.
    1982 Analysis of the Preservation of Community Structure in Assemblages of Fossil Mammals. *Paleobiology* 8: 434-446.
284. Dapples, E. C.
    1942 The Effects of Macro-Organisms Upon Near-Shore Marine Sediments. *Journal of Sedimentary Petrology* 12: 118-126.
285. Dart, R. A.
    1949 The Predatory Implemental Technique of Australopithecus. *American Journal of Physical Anthropology* 7: 1-38.
286. Dart, R. A.
    1953 The Predatory Transition from Ape to Man. *International Anthropological and Linguistic Review* 1: 201-218.
287. Dart, R. A.
    1956 The Myth of the Bone-Accumulating Hyena. *American Anthropologist* 58: 40-62.
288. Dart, R. A.
    1957 An Australopithecine Object from Makapansgat. *Nature* 179: 693-695.
289. Dart, R. A.
    1957 *The Osteodontokeratic Culture of Australopithecus Prometheus*. Transvaal Museum, Pretoria. Memoris No. 10.
290. Dart, R. A.
    1957 The Makapansgat Australopithecus Osteodontokeratic Culture. In *Proceedings of the 3rd Pan-African Congress on Prehistory*, edited by J. D. Clark, pp. 161-171. Chatto and Windus, London.
291. Dart, R. A.
    1958 Bone Tools and Porcupine Gnawing. *American Anthropologist* 60: 715-724.
292. Dart, R. A.
    1958 The Minimal Bone-Breccia Content of Makapansgat and the Australopithecine Predatory Habit. *American Anthropologist* 60: 923-931.
293. Dart, R. A.
    1959 Osteodontokeratic Ripping Tools and Pulp Scoops for Teething and Edentulous Australopithecines. *Dental Association of South Africa. Journal* 14: 164-178.
294. Dart, R. A.
    1959 An Australopithecine Scoop from Herefordshire. *Nature* 183: 844.
295. Dart, R. A.
    1959 Further Light on Australopithecus Humeral and Femoral Weapons. *American Journal of Physical Anthropology* 17: 87-94.
296. Dart, R. A.
    1959 Cannon-Bone Scoops and Daggers. *South African Journal of Science* 55: 79-82.
297. Dart, R. A.
    1960 The Bone Tool-Manufacturing Ability of *Australopithecus prometheus*. *American Anthropologist* 62: 134-143.
298. Dart, R. A.
    1960 The Persistence of Some Tools and Utensils Found First in the Makapansgat Gray Breccia. *South African Journal of Science* 56: 71-74.

299. Dart, R. A.
1961 An Australopithecine Scoop Made from a Right Australopithecine Upper Arm Bone. *Nature* 191: 372-373.

300. Dart, R. A.
1961 Futher Information About How Australopithecus Made Bone Tools and Utensils. *South African Journal of Science* 57: 127-134.

301. Dart, R. A.
1962 The Continuity and Originality of Australopithecine Osteodontokeratic Culture. In *4e Congres Pan-African du Prehistoire et de l'Etude Quaternaire, Actes* pp. 27-40. Annales, Serie in 80: Sciences Humaines, No. 40. Musee Royale de l'Afrique Central, Tervuren, Belgium.

302. Dart, R. A.
1962 From Cannon-Bone Scoops to Skull Bowls at Makapansgat. *American Journal of Physical Anthropology* 20: 287-296.

303. Dart, R. A.
1964 The Abbe Breuil and the Osteodontokeratic Culture. In *Miscelanea en Homenaje al Abate Henri Breuil, 1877-1961*, vol. 1, edited by E. Ripoll Perello, pp. 348-361. Instituto de Prehistoria y Arqueologia, Barcelona.

304. Dart, R. A.
1965 The Ecology of the South African Man-Apes. *Monographiae Biologicae* 14: 49-66.

305. Dart, R. A.
1965 Tree Chopping with an Elephant Rib. *South African Journal of Science* 61: 395-396.

306. Dart, R. A., and J. W. Kitching
1958 Bone Tools at the Kalkbank Middle Stone Age Site and the Makapansgat Australopithecine Locality, Central Transvaal. Part 2: The Osteodontokeratic Contribution. *South African Archaeological Bulletin* 13: 94-116.

307. Darwin, C. R.
1881 *The Formation of Vegetable Mould Through the Action of Worms with Observations on Their Habits*. John Murray, London.

308. Das, S. K., and R. S. Harris
1966 Fatty Acids in Fossil Teeth (Abstract). *International Association for Dental Research. 44th General Meeting. Program and Abstracts of Papers*, p. 67.

309. Das, S. K., A. R. Doberenz, and R. W. G. Wyckoff
1967 The Lipids in Fossils. *Comparative Biochemistry and Physiology* 23: 519-525.

310. Davidson, F. D., J. P. Lehman, P. Taquet, and R. W. G. Wyckoff
1978 Analyse des Protéines de Vertébrés Fossiles Dévoniens et Crétacés du Sahara. *Academie des Sciences, Paris. Comptes Rendus Hebdomadaires des Séances*, Series D, 287: 919-922. Paris.

311. Davis, D. D., T. R. Kidder, and D. R. Barondess
1983 Reduction Analysis of Sample Bone Industries: An example from the Louisiana Coastal Zone. *Archaeology of Eastern North America* 11: 98-108.

312. De Ploey, J.
1964 Nappes de Gravats et Couvertures Argilo-Sableuses au Bas-Congo: Leur Genese et l'Action des Termites. In *Etudes sur les Termites Africains*, edited by Albert Bouillon, pp. 399-414. Studia Universitatis "Lovanium," Faculte des Sciences No. 15. Editions de L'Université, Leopolville.

313. De Ploey, J.
1965 Position Géomorphologique, Génèet Chronologie de Certains Dépôts Superficiels au Congo Occidental. *Quaternaria* 7: 131-154.

314. De Ploey, J., and J. Moeyersons
1975 Runoff Creep of Coarse Debris: Experimental Data and Some Field Observations. *Catena* 2: 275-288.

315. De Vis, C. W.
1883 On Tooth-Marked Bones of Extinct Marsupials. *Linnean Society of New South Wales. Proceedings* 8: 187-190.

316. De Vis, C. W.
1899 Remarks on a Fossil Implement and Bones of an Extinct Kangaroo. *Royal Society of Victoria. Proceedings* 12: 81-90.

317. De Vis, C. W.
1900 Bones and Diet of Thylacoleo. *Queensland Museum, Brisbane. Annals* 5: 7-11.

318. Dechant-Boaz, D. E.
1982 Preliminary Assessment of Taphonomy and Paleoecology at Sahabi. *Garyounis Scientific Bulletin* Special Issue No. 4: 109-121. University of Garyounis, Behyhazi, Libya.

319. Dechant-Boaz, D. E.
1982 *Modern Riverine Taphonomy: Its Relevance to the Interpretation of Plio-Pleistocene Hominid Paleoecology in the Omo Basin, Ethiopia*. Ph.D. dissertation, University of California, Berkeley. University Microfilms 8312762, Ann Arbor.

320. Deevey, E. S.
1947 Life Tables for Natural Populations of Animals. *Quaterly Review of Biology* 22: 283-314.

321. Demere, T. A., and R. A. Cerutti
1982 A Pliocene Shark Attack in a Cetotheiid Whale. *Journal of Paleontology* 56: 1480-1482.

322. Dence, W. A.
1956 Concretions of the Alewife, *Pomolobus pseudoharengus* (Wilson), at Onondaga Lake, New York. *Copeia* 3: 155-158.

323. Dibble, D. S., and D. Lorrain
1968 *Bonfire Shelter: A Stratified Bison Kill Site, Val Verde County, Texas*. Texas Memorial Museum, Austin. Miscellaneous Papers No. 1.

324. Dietz, E. F.
1955 Natural Burial of Artifacts. *American Antiquity* 20: 273-274.

325. Dincauze, D. F.
1968 Cremation Cemeteries in Eastern Massachusetts. *Peabody Museum of Archaeology and Ethnology. Papers* 59: 1-1-3.

326. Dixon, E. J.
    1984 Context and Environment in Taphonomic Analysis: Examples from Alaska's Porcupine River Caves. *Quaternary Research* 22: 201-215.
327. Dixon, E. J., and R. M. Thorson
    1984 Taphonomic Analysis and Interpretation in North American Pleistocene Archaeology. *Quaternary Research* 22: 155-159.
328. Doberenz, A. R., and R. Lund
    1966 Evidence for Collagen in a Fossil of the Lower Jurassic. *Nature* 212: 1502-1503.
329. Doberenz, A. R., and R. W. G. Wyckoff
    1967 Fine Structure in Fossil Collagen. *National Academy of Sciences, Washington, D. C. Proceedings* 57: 539-541.
330. Doberenz, A. R., M. F. Miller, and R. W. G. Wyckoff
    1969 An Analysis of Fossil Enamel Protein. *Calcified Tissue Research* 3: 93-95.
331. Dodd, J. R., and R. J. Stanton, Jr.
    1981 Fossils as Sedimentary Particles. In *Paleoecology: Concepts and Applications*, pp. 299-336. Wiley-Interscience, New York.
332. Dodds, D. G.
    1955 Food Habits of the Newfoundland Red Fox. *Journal of Mammalogy* 36: 291.
333. Dodson, P.
    1971 Sedimentology and Taphonomy of the Oldman Formation (Campanian), Dinosaur Provincial Park, Alberta (Canada). *Palaeogeography, Palaeoclimatology, Palaeoecology* 10: 21-74.
334. Dodson, P.
    1973 The Significance of Small Bones in Paleoecological Interpretation. *Contributions to Geology* 12: 15-19.
335. Dodson, P.
    1980 Vertebrate Burials. *Paleobiology* 6: 6-8.
336. Dodson, P., Behrensmeyer, A. K., and R. T. Baker
    1980 Taphonomy of the Morrison Formation (Kimmeridgian-Portlandian) and Cloverly Formation (Aptian-Albain) of the Western United States. *Société Géologique de France. Mémoires*, New Series, 139: 87-93.
337. Dodson, P., and D. Wexlar
    1979 Taphonomic Investigations of Owl Pellets. *Paleobiology* 5: 275-284.
338. Dortch, C. E.
    1974 A Twelve Thousand Year Old Occupation Floor in Devil's Lair, Western Australia. *Mankind* 9: 195-205.
339. Dortch, C. E.
    1979 33,000 Year Old Stone and Bone Artifacts from Devil's Lair, Western Australia. *Western Australian Museum. Records* 7: 329-367. Perth.
340. Dortch, C. E.
    1979 Devil's Lair, an Example of Prolonged Cave Use in Southwestern Australia. *World Archaeology* 10: 258-279.
341. Dortch, C. E., and D. Merrilees
    1971 A Salvage Excavation in Devil's Lair, Western Australia. *Royal Society of Western Australia. Journal* 54: 103-113.
342. Dortch, C. E., and D. Merrilees
    1973 Human Occupation of Devil's Lair, Western Australia During the Pleistocene. *Archaeology and Physical Anthropology in Oceania* 8: 89-115.
343. Douglas, A. M., G. W. Kendrick, and D. Merrilees
    1966 A Fossil Deposit near Perth, Western Australia, Interpreted as a Carnivore's Den After Feeding Tests on Living *Sarcophilus* (Marsupiala, Dasyuridae). *Royal Society of Western Australia. Journal* 49: 88-90.
344. Douglas-Hamilton, I.
    1972 *On the Ecology and Behaviour of the African Elephant*. Ph.D. thesis, University of Oxford.
345. Douglas-Hamilton, I., and O. Douglas-Hamilton
    1975 *Among the Elephants*. Harvill Press, London.
346. Driesch, A. von den
    1976 *A Guide to the Measurement of Animal Bones from Archaeological Sites*. Peabody Museum of Archaeology and Ethnology. Bulletin No. 1.
347. Driscoll, E. G.
    1967 Experimental Field Study of Shell Abrasion. *Journal of Sedimentary Petrology* 37: 1117-1123.
348. Driscoll, E. G., and T. P. Weltin
    1973 Sedimentary Parameters as Factors in Abrasive Shell Reduction. *Palaeogeography, Palaeoclimatology, Palaeoecology* 3: 275-288.
349. Driver, J. C.
    1982 Early Prehistoric Killing of Bighorn Sheep in the Southeastern Canadian Rockies. *Plains Anthropologist* 27: 265-271.
350. Driver, J. C.
    1983 Bison Death Assemblages and Communal Hunting. In *Carnivores, Human Scavengers and Predators*, edited by G. M. LeMoine and A. S. MacEachern, pp. 141-155. (15th Annual Chacmool Conference, Proceedings). Archaeological Association, Department of Archaeology, University of Calgary, Alberta.
351. Driver, J. C.
    1983 Review of *The Hunters or the Hunted?*, by C. K. Brain. *Zooarchaeological Research News* 2(4): 9-10.
352. Dubiel, R. F.
    1987 Sedimentology of the Upper Triassic Chinle Formation, Southeastern Utah: Paleoclimatic Implications. *Arizona-Nevada Academy of Science. Journal* 22: 35-45.
353. Dubiel, R. F., R. H. Blodgett, and T. M. Bown
    1987 Lungfish Burrows in the Upper Triassic Chinle and Dolores Formations, Colorado Plateau. *Journal of Sedimentary Petrology* 57: 512-521.
354. Dubois, E.
    1927 Über die Hauptmerkmale des Femur von *Pithecanthropus erectus*. *Anthropologischer Anzeiger* 4: 131-146.
355. Duckworth, W. L. H.
    1904 Note on the Dispersive Power of Running Water on Skeletons: With Particular Reference to the Skeletal Remains of *Pithecanthropus erectus*. In *Studies from the Anthropological Laboratory*, The Anatomy School, Cambridge, edited by W. L. H. Duckworth, pp. 274-277. Cambridge University Press, Cambridge.

356. Ducos, P.
    1984 La Contribution de L'Archeozoologie a L'Estimation des Quantities de Nourriture: Evaluation du Nombre Initial D'Individus. In *Animals and Archaeology: 3. Early Herders and Their Flocks*, edited by J. Clutton-Brock and C. Grigson, pp. 13-23. British Archaeological Reports, BAR International Series No. 202. Oxford.
357. Duke, G. E., O. A. Evanson, and A. A. Jegers
    1976 Meal to Pellet Intervals in 14 Species of Captive Raptors. *Comparative Biochemistry and Physiology* 53A: 1-6.
358. Duke, G. E., A. A. Jegers, G. Loff, and O. A. Evanson
    1975 Gastric Digestion in Some Raptors. *Comparative Biochemistry and Physiology* 50A: 649-656.
359. Dumond, D. E.
    1982 Reviews and Book Abstracts: Colonization of the American Arctic and the New World. (Reviews of *Pleistocene Bone Technology*, by R. Bonnichsen, and *Taphonomy and Archaeology*, by R. E. Morlan). *American Antiquity* 47: 885-895.
360. Dunbar, J. S., S. D. Webb, and D. Cring
    1989 Culturally and Naturally Modified Bones from a Paleo-Indian Site in the Aucilla River, North Florida. In *Bone Modification*, edited by R. Bonnichsen and M. Sorg (1st International Bone Modification Conference, Proceedings). Center for the Study of the First Americans, Orono, Maine.
361. Durham, J. W.
    1967 The Incompleteness of our Knowledge of the Fossil Record. *Journal of Paleontology* 41: 559-565.
362. Eastoe, J. E., and B. Eastoe
    1954 The Organic Constituents of Mammalian Compact Bone. *Biochemical Journal* 57: 453-459.
363. Efremov, I. A.
    1940 Taphonomy: A New Branch of Paleontology. *Pan-American Geologist* 74: 81-93.
364. Efremov, I. A.
    1950 *Tafonomiia i Geologicheskaiia Letopis*. (Taphonomy and the Geological Record). Akademiia Nauk, USSR Paleontologicheskii Institut. Trudy 24.
365. Efremov, I. A.
    1953 *Taphonomie et Annales Géologiques* (French translation of Efremov 1950). Translated by S. Ketchian and J. Roger. Centre d'Études de Documentation Paléontologiques, Annales No. 4. Paris.
366. Efremov, I. A.
    1957 On the Taphonomy of Fossil Faunas of Terrestrial Vertebrates of Mongolia (in Russian with English summary). *Ku Chi Ch'ui Tung Wu Hsueh Pao (Vertebrata Palasiatica)* 1: 83-102.
367. Efremov, I. A.
    1958 Some Consideration in the Biological Bases of Paleozoology. *Ku Chi Ch'ui Tung Wu Hsueh Pao (Vertebrata Palasiatica)* 2: 83-99.
368. Einarsen, A. S.
    1956 *Determination of Some Predator Species by Field Signs*. Oregon State Monographs. Studies in Zoology No. 10.
369. Elder, R. L.
    1987 Taphonomy and Paleoecology of the Dockum Group, Howard County, Texas. *Arizona-Nevada Academy of Science. Journal* 22: 85-94.
370. Eloff, F. C.
    1964 On the Predatory Habits of Lions and Hyaenas. *Koedoe* 7: 105-112.
371. Eloff, F. C.
    1973 Lion Predation in the Kalahari Gemsbok National Park. *South African Wildlife Management Association. Journal* 3: 59-63.
372. Enlow, D. H.
    1963 *Principles of Bone Remodeling*. C. C. Thomas, Springfield, Illinois.
373. Enlow, D. H., and S. O. Brown
    1956 A Comparative Histological Study of Fossil and Recent Bone Tissues. Part 1. *Texas Journal of Science* 8: 405-443.
374. Enlow, D. H., and S. O. Brown
    1957 A Comparative Histological Study of Fossil and Recent Bone Tissues. Part 2. *Texas Journal of Science* 9: 186-214.
375. Ericson, J. E.
    1985 Strontium Isotope Characterization in the Study of Preshitoric Human Ecology. *Journal of Human Evolution* 14: 503-514.
376. Ericson, Per G. P.
    1987 Interpretations of Archaeological Bird Remains: A Taphonomic Approach. *Journal of Archaeological Science* 14: 65-75.
377. Erlandson, J. M.
    1984 A Case Study in Faunalturbation: Delineating the Effects of the Burrowing Pocket Gopher on the Distribution of Archaeological Remains. *American Antiquity* 49: 785-790.
378. Evans, A. C.
    1948 Studies on the Relationships Between Earthworms and Soil Fertility: 2. Some Effects of Earthworms on Soil Structures. *Annals of Applied Biology* 35: 1-13.
379. Evans, E. M. N.
    1970 The Reaction of a Group of Rothschild's Giraffe to a New Environment. *East African Wildlife Journal* 8: 53-62.
380. Evans, F. C., and J. T. Emlem, Jr.
    1947 Ecological Notes on the Prey Selected by a Barn Owl. *Condor* 49: 3-9.
381. Evans, F. G.
    1957 *Stress and Strain in Bones*. C. C. Thomas, Springfield, Illinois.
382. Evans, F. G.
    1961 Relation of the Physical Properties of Bone to Fractures. *American Academy of Orthopedic Surgeons. Instructional Course Lectures* 18: 110-121.
383. Evans, F. G.
    1973 *Mechanical Properties of Bone*. C. C. Thomas, Springfield, Illinois.
384. Everts, J. M., A. R. Doberenz, and R. W. G. Wyckoff
    1968 Fatty Acids in Fossil Bones. *Comparative Biochemistry and Physiology* 6: 955-962.

385. Ewer, R. F.
1954 Some Adaptive Features in the Dentition of Hyenas. *Annals and Magazine of Natural History*, Series 12, 7: 185-194.

386. Ewer, R. F.
1967 The Fossil Hyaenids of Africa: A Reappraisal. In *Background to Evolution in Africa*, edited by W. W. Bishop and J. D. Clark, pp. 109-123. University of Chicago Press, Chicago.

387. Fagerstrom, J. A.
1964 Fossil Communities in Paleoecology: Their Recognition and Significance. *Geological Society of America. Bulletin* 75: 1197-1216.

388. Fahnestock, R. K., and W. L. Haushild
1962 Flume Studies of Transport of Pebbles and Cobbles on a Sand Bed. *Geological Society of America. Bulletin* 73: 1431-1436.

389. Falk, C. R.
1977 Analyses of Unmodified Vertebrate Fauna from Sites in the Middle Missouri Subarea: A Review. *Plains Anthropologist* 22: 150-161.

390. Fay, F. H., and B. P. Kelly
1980 Mass Mortality of Walrus *(Odobenus rosmarus)* at St. Lawrence Island, Bering Sea, Autumn, 1978. *Arctic* 33: 226-245.

391. Fichter, E., G. Schildman, and J. H. Sather
1955 Some Feeding Patterns of Coyotes in Nebraska. *Ecological Monographs* 25: 1-37.

392. Fieller, N. R. J., and A. Turner
1982 Number Estimation in Vertebrate Samples. *Journal of Archaeological Science* 9: 49-62.

393. Fiorillo, A. R.
1989 An Experimental Study of Trampling: Implications for the Fossil Record. In *Bone Modification*, edited by R. Bonnichsen and M. Sorg (1st International Bone Modification Conference, Proceedings). Center for the Study of the First Americans, Orono, Maine.

394. Fisher, D. C.
1981 Evidence of Mastodon Butchering in Southeastern Michigan. Geological Society of America, abstracts with programs 13: 452.

395. Fisher, D. C.
1981 Mode of Preservation of the Shotgun Local Fauna (Paleocene, Wyoming) and its Implication for the Taphonomy of a Microvertebrate Concentration. *University of Michigan, Ann Arbor, Museum of Paleontology. Contributions* 25: 247-257.

396. Fisher, D. C.
1981 Crocodilian Scatology, Microvertebra Concentrations, and Enamel-less Teeth. *Paleobiology* 7: 262-275.

397. Fisher, D. C.
1981 Taphonomic Interpretation of Enamel-less Teeth in the Shotgun Local Fauna (Paleocene, Wyoming). *University of Michigan, Ann Arbor, Museum of Paleontology. Contributions* 25: 259-275.

398. Fisher, D. C.
1984 Mastodon Butchery by North American Paleo-Indians. *Nature* 308: 271-272.

399. Fisunenko, O. P.
1978 Tafonomiya i Infrafatsii (Taphonomy and Interfacies; in Russian). In *Voprosy Tafonomii i Paleobiologii*, Chaired by B. S. Soklov, pp. 165-173. SSSR, Akademiya Nauk, Vsesoyuznoe Paleontologicheskoe Obvshchestvo. Trudy Sessi 20. Leningrad.

400. Fleming, R. L.
1955 Bone-dropping Habit of the Lammergeier. *Bombay Natural History Society. Journal* 52: 933-935.

401. Flinn, R. M., M. E. Corbett, and A. J. Smith
1987 An Unusual Dental Deposit — A Taphonomic Process? *Journal of Archaeological Science* 14: 291-295.

402. Floyd, T. J., L. D. Mech, and P. A. Jordan
1978 Relating Wolf Scat Content to Prey Consumed. *Journal of Wildlife Management* 42: 528-532.

403. Foley, R.
1981 Off-site Archaeology and Human Adaptation in Eastern Africa. *Monographs in African Archaeology*, No. 3. British Archaeological Reports, BAR International Series No. 97. Oxford.

404. Foley, R.
1983 Modelling Hunting Strategies and Inferring Predator Behaviour from Prey Attributes. In *Animals and Archaeology: 1. Hunters and Their Prey*, edited by J. Clutton-Brock and C. Grigson, pp. 63-75. British Archaeological Reports, BAR International Series No. 163. Oxford.

405. Folk, R. L.
1968 *Petrology of Sedimentary Rocks*. Hemphill's, Austin, Tex.

406. Forbes, G.
1941 The Effects of Heat on the Histological Structure of Bone. *Police Journal* 14: 50-60.

407. Forbis, R. G.
1960 The Old Woman's Buffalo Jump, Alberta. *National Museum of Canada. Bulletin* No. 180: 57-123. (Contributions to Anthropology, 1960, Paper No. 1).

408. Freeman, L. G.
1978 Mousterian Worked Bone from Cueva Morin (Santander, Spain): A Preliminary Description. In *Views of the Past*, edited by L. G. Freeman, pp. 29-51. Mouton, The Hague.

409. Freeman, L. G.
1983 More on the Mousterian: Flaked Bone from Cueva Morin. (Review of *Bones*, by L. R. Binford). *Current Anthropology* 24: 366-372.

410. Frison, G. C.
1970 *The Glenrock Buffalo Jump, 48CO304*. Plains Anthropologist. Memoir No. 7.

411. Frison, G. C.
1971 The Bison Pound in Northwestern Plains Prehistory. *American Antiquity* 36: 77-91.

412. Frison, G. C.
1972 Evidence for Use on Bone Tool Assemblages from Plains *Bison* and *Bison antiquus* Butchering Sites. Paper read at the 37th annual meeting of the Society for American Archaeology, Bal Harbor, Florida.

413. Frison, G. C.
    1973 *The Wardell Buffalo Trap 48SU301: Communal Procurement in the Upper Green River Basin, Wyoming.* University of Michigan, Ann Arbor. Anthropological Papers No. 48.
414. Frison, G. C.
    1976 Cultural Activity Associated with Prehistoric Mammoth Butchering and Processing. *Science* 194: 728-730.
415. Frison, G. C.
    1978 *Prehistoric Hunters of the High Plains.* Academic Press, New York.
416. Frison, G. C.
    1982 Bone Butchering Tools in Archaeological Sites. *Canadian Journal of Anthropology* 2: 159-167.
417. Frison, G. C. (editor)
    1974 *The Casper Site: A Hell Gap Bison Kill on the High Plains.* Academic Press, New York.
418. Frison, G. C., D. N. Walker, S. D. Webb, and G. M. Zeimens
    1978 Paleo-Indian Procurement of *Camelops* on the Northwestern Plains. *Quaternary Research* 10: 385-400.
419. Frison, G. C., and G. M. Zeimens
    1980 Bone Projectile Points: An Addition to the Folsom Cultural Complex. *American Antiquity* 45: 231-237.
420. Fuchs, C., D. Faufman, and A. Ronen
    1977 Erosion and Artifact Distribution in Open-Air Epi-Palaeolithic Sites on the Coastal Plain of Israel. *Journal of Field Archaeology* 4: 171-179.
421. Fürsich, F. T.
    1978 The Influence of Faunal Condensation and Mixing on the Preservation of Fossil Benthic Communities. *Lethaia* 11: 243-250.
422. Fürsich, F. T.
    1978 Variability of Jurassic Hardground Faunas: Pitfalls in Studies of Community Evolution. *Neues Jahrbuch für und Paläontologie. Abhandlugen* 157: 52-56.
423. Futterer, E.
    1978 Hydrodynamic Behavior of Biogenic Particles. *Neues Jahrbuch für Geologie und Paläontologie. Abhandlugen* 157: 37-42.
424. Galdikas, B. M. F.
    1978 Orangutan Death and Scavenging by Pigs. *Science* 200: 68-70.
425. Galdikas, B. M. F., and C. P. Yeager
    1984 Crocodile Predation on a Crab-eating Macaque in Borneo. *American Journal of Primatology* 6: 49-51.
426. Gashwiler, J. S., W. L. Robinette, and O. W. Morris
    1960 Foods of Bobcats in Utah and Eastern Nevada. *Journal of Wildlife Management* 24: 226-229.
427. Gautier, A., and H. Schumann
    1973 Puparia of the Subarctic or Black Blowfly, *Protophormia terraenovae*, (Robineau-Desvoidy, 1830) in a Skull of a Late Eemian (?) Bison at Zemst, Brabant (Belgium). *Palaeogeography, Palaeoclimatology, Palaeoecology* 14: 119-125.
428. Gautier, A., and V. Rubberechts
    1976 Animal Remains of the Senecaberg Fortification. *Musées Royaux d'Art et d'Histoire, Brussels. Bulletin* 48: 49-84.
429. Gavrilishin, V. I.
    1978 Kharakter Zakhoroneniya i Sokhrannoct Ostatkov Organizmov v Mezoroiskikh Otlozheniykh Zapada Ukrainy (The Burial and Preservation of the Remains of Living Organisms in Mesozoic Deposits of the Western Ukraine; in Russian). In *Voprosy Tafonomii i Paleobiologii*, Chaired by B. S. Soklov, pp. 153-157. SSSR, Akademiya Nauk, Vsesoyuznoe Paleontologicheskoe Obshchestvo. Trudy Sessi 20. Leningrad.
430. Gebo, D. L., and E. L. Simons
    1984 Puncture Marks on Early African Anthropoids. *American Journal of Physical Anthropology* 65: 31-35.
431. Gekker, R. F.
    1965 *Introduction to Paleoecology.* American Elsevier, New York.
432. Gentry, A. W.
    1970 The Bovidae (Mammalia) of the Fort Ternan Fossil Fauna. In *Fossil Vertebrates of Africa*, vol. 3, pp. 243-323. Academic Press, New York.
433. Gifford, D. P.
    1977 *Observations of Modern Human Settlements as an Aid to Archaeological Interpretation.* Ph. D. dissertation, University of California, Berkeley. University Microfilms 7812572, Ann Arbor.
434. Gifford, D. P.
    1978 Ethnoarchaeological Observations of Natural Processes Affecting Cultural Materials. In *Explorations in Ethnoarchaeology*, edited by R. A. Gould, pp. 77-101. University of New Mexico Press, Albuquerque.
435. Gifford, D. P.
    1980 Ethnoarcheological Contributions to the Taphonomy of Human Sites. In *Fossils in the Making: Vertebrate Taphonomy and Paleoecology*, edited by A. K. Behersmeyer and A. P. Hill, pp. 93-106.
436. Gifford, D. P.
    1981 Taphonomy and Paleoecology: A Critical Review of Archaeology's Sister Disciplines. In *Advances in Archaeological Method and Theory*, vol. 4, edited by M. B. Schiffer, pp. 365-438. Academic Press, New York.
437. Gifford, D. P.
    1982 *Australopithecus* and Predation: Review of *The Hunters or the Hunted? Science* 215: 154-155.
438. Gifford, D. P., and A. K. Behrensmeyer
    1977 Observed Formation and Burial of a Recent Human Occupation Site in Kenya. *Quaternary Research* 8: 245-266.
439. Gifford, D. P., and D. C. Crader
    1977 A Computer Coding System for Archaeological Remains. *American Antiquity* 42: 225-238.
440. Gifford, D. P., G. L. Isaac, and C. M. Nelson
    1980 Evidence for predation and pastoralism at Prolonged Drift: A Pastoral Neolithic site in Kenya. *Azania* 15: 57-108.

441. Gifford-Gonzalez, D. P.
    1984 Hunt for Nutrition (Review of *Bison Kills and Bone Counts*, by J. D. Speth). *Nature* 308: 88.
442. Gifford-Gonzalez, D. P.
    1984 Implications of a Faunal Assemblage Pastoral Neolithic Site in Kenya: Findings and a Perspective on Research. In *From Hunters to Farmers*, edited by J. D. Clark and S. A. Brandt, pp. 240-251. University of California Press, Berkeley.
443. Gifford-Gonzalez, D. P.
    1989 Modern Analogues: Developing an Interpretive Framework. In *Bone Modification*, edited by R. Bonnichsen and M. Sorg (1st International Bone Modification Conference, Proceedings). Center for the Study of the First Americans, Orono, Maine.
444. Gifford-Gonzalez, D. P.
    1989 Ethnographic Analogues for Interpreting Modified Bones: The View from East Africa. In *Bone Modification*, edited by R. Bonnichsen and M. Sorg (1st International Bone Modification Conference, Proceedings). Center for the Study of the First Americans, Orono, Maine.
445. Gifford-Gonzalez, D. P., D. B. Damrosch, D. R. Damrosch, J. Pryor and R. L. Thunen
    1985 The Third Dimension in Site Structure: An Experiment in Trampling and Vertical Dispersal. *American Antiquity* 50: 803-818.
446. Gifford-Gonzalez, D. P., G. L. Isaac, and C. M. Nelson
    1980 Evidence for Predation and Pastoralism at Prolonged Drift: A Pastoral Neolithic Site in Kenya. *Azania* 15: 57-108.
447. Gilbert, A. S.
    1979 *Urban Taphonomy of Mammalian Remains from the Bronze Age of Godin Tepe, Western Iran*. Ph.D. dissertation, Columbia University. University Microfilms 8008727, Ann Arbor.
448. Gilbert, A. S., and B. H. Singer
    1982 Reassessing Zooarchaeological Quantification. *World Archaeology* 14: 21-40.
449. Gilbert, A. S., and P. Steinfeld
    1977 Faunal Remains from Dinkha Tepe, Northwestern Iran. *Journal of Field Archaeology* 4: 329-351.
450. Gilbert, B. M.
    1969 Some Aspects of Diet and Butchering Techniques Among Prehistoric Indians in South Dakota. *Plains Anthropologist* 14: 277-294.
451. Gilbert, B. M., and W. M. Bass
    1967 Seasonal Dating of Burials from the Presence of Fly Pupae. *American Antiquity* 32: 534-535.
452. Gill, E. D.
    1952 Thylacoleo and Incised Bone. *Australian Journal of Science* 14: 201.
453. Gill, E. D.
    1968 Paleoecology of Fossil Human Skeletons. *Palaeogeography, Palaeoclimatology, Palaeoecology* 4: 211-217.
454. Ginda, V. A.
    1978 Uslovya Zakhoroneniya i Sokhrannost Iskopaemykh Ostatkov v Ordovike Volyni (Conditions for the Burial and Preservation of Fossil Remains in the Oldovician of Volyn; in Russian). In *Voprosy Tafonomii i Paleobiologii*, Chaired by B. S. Soklov, pp. 65-66. SSSR, Akademiya Nauk, Vseoyuzhoe Paleontologicheskoe Obshchestvo. Trudy Sessi 20. Leningrad.
455. Gladfelter, B. G.
    1977 Geoarchaeology: The Geomorphologist and Archaeology. *American Antiquity* 42: 519-538.
456. Gladkih, M. I., N. L. Kornietz, and O. Soffer
    1984 Mammoth-bone Dwellings in the Russian Plain. *Scientific American* 251: 164-175.
457. Glimcher, M. J.
    1960 Specificity of the Molecular Structure of Organic Matrices in Mineralization. In *Calcification in Biological Systems*, edited by R. F. Sognnaes, pp. 421-487. American Association for the Advancement of Science. Publications No. 64.
458. Glover, P. E., E. C. Glover, T. E. Trump, and L. E. D. Waterridge
    1964 The Lava Caves of Mt. Suswa, Kenya. *Studies in Speleology* 1: 51-66.
459. Glue, D. E.
    1970 Avian Predator Pellet Analysis and the Mammalogist. *Mammal Review* 1: 53-62.
460. Goldberg, P.
    1985 Comment on Binford and Ho 1985 (Reply by Binford and Ho). *Current Anthropology* 26: 431-432.
461. Goodard, C. B.
    1958 Thrush Predation on the Snail *Cepaea hortensis*. *Journal of Animal Ecology* 27: 47-57.
462. Goretskiy, V. A., and Z. I. Khmelevskiy
    1978 K Paleoekologii Mela i Miostena Yugo-zapadnoi Okrainy Vostochno-Evropeiskoi Platformy (Cretaceous and Miocene Paleoecology of the Southwestern Regions of the Russian Platform; in Russian). In *Voprosy Tafonomii i Paleobiologii*, Chaired by B. S. Soklov, pp. 69-75. SSSR, Akademiya Sessi 20. Leningrad.
463. Gordon, B. C.
    1976 Antler Pseudo-Tools Made from Caribou. In *Primitive Art and Technology*, edited by J. S. Raymond, B. Loveseth, C. Arnold, and G. Reardon, pp. 121-128. (Symposium on Primitive Technology and Art, Calgary, Alberta, 1974). Archaeological Association, Department of Archaeology, University of Calgary, Alberta.
464. Gordon, C. C., and J. E. Buikstra
    1981 Soil pH, Bone Preservation and Sampling Bias at Mortuary Sites. *American Antiquity* 46: 566-571.
465. Gould, R. A.
    1980 *Living Archaeology*. Cambridge University Press, Cambridge.

466. Gow, C. E.
    1973 Habitual Sheltering in an Extensive Cave System by Baboons Near Bredasdorp, South Africa. *South African Journal of Science* 69: 182.
467. Gradzinski, R.
    1969 Sedimentation of Dinosaur-Bearing Upper Cretaceous Deposits of the Nemegt Basin, Gobi Desert. *Palaeontologica Polonica* 21: 147-229.
468. Graham, A. D., and R. M. Laws
    1971 The Collection of Found Ivory in Murchison Fall National Park. *East African Wildlife Journal* 9: 57-65.
469. Graham, R. W., J. A. Holman, and P. W. Parmalee
    1983 *Taphonomy and Paleoecology of the Christensen Bog Mastadon Bone Bed, Hancock County, Indiana*. Reports of Investigations Series No. 38. Illinois State Musuem.
470. Grant, P., and C. Ekland
    1977 Discriminant Analysis of Fragments from Long Bone Diaphyses. Paper presented at the annual meeting of the Society for American Archaeology, New Orleans.
471. Grassé, P-P.
    1950 Termites et Sols Tropicaux. *Revue Internationale de Botanique Apliquée et d'Agriculture Tropicale*. 30: 549-554.
472. Gratacap, L. P.
    1896 Fossils and Fossilization. *American Naturalist* 30: 902-912.
473. Grayson, D. K.
    1978 Minimum Numbers and Sample Size in Vertebrate Faunal Analysis. *American Antiquity* 43: 53-65.
474. Grayson, D. K.
    1978 Reconstructing Mammalian Communitites: A Discussion of Shotwell's Method of Paleoecological Analysis. *Paleobiology* 4: 77-81.
475. Grayson, D. K.
    1979 On the Quantification of Vertebrate Archaeofaunas. In *Advances in Archaeological Method and Theory*, vol. 2, edited by M. B. Schiffer, pp. 199-237. Academic Press, New York.
476. Grayson, D. K.
    1982 Review of *Bones*, by L. R. Binford. *American Anthropologist* 84: 439-440.
477. Grayson, D. K.
    1984 *Quantitive Zooarchaeology: Topics in the Analysis of Archaeological Faunas*. Academic Press, New York.
478. Green, R. H.
    1979 Matrix Population Models Applied to Living Populations and Death Assemblages. *American Journal of Science* 279: 481-487.
479. Gregory, J. T., J. A. Bacskai, B. Brajnikov, and K. Munthe
    1973 *Bibliography of Fossil Vertebrates, 1969-1972*. Geological Society of America. Memoirs 141.
480. Gregory, J. T., J. A. Bacskai, and G. V. Shkurkin
    1978 *Bibliography of Fossil Vertebrates, 1978*. American Geological Institute, Society of Vertebrate Paleontology.
481. Gregory, J. T., J. A. Bacskai, G. V. Shkurkin, and L. A. Bryant
    1981 *Bibliography of Fossil Vertebrates, 1979*. American Geological Institute, Society of Vertebrate Paleontology.
482. Grigson, C.
    1983 Review of: *Bones: Ancient Men and Modern Myths*, by L. R. Binford. *Journal of Archaeological Science* 11: 296-297.
483. Grinnell, J.
    1923 The Burrowing Rodents of California as Agents in Soil Formation. *Journal of Mammalogy* 4: 137-149.
484. Grobler, J. H., and V. J. Wilson
    1970 Food of the Leopard *Panthera pardus* (Linn.) in the Rhodes Matopos National Park, Rhodesia, as Determined by Faecal Analysis. *Arnoldia* 5(35): 1-10.
485. Grønnow, B., M. Meldgaard, and B. Nielsen
    1983 Aasivissuit — The Great Summer Camp: Archaeological, Ethnographical and Zoo-archaeological Studies of a Caribou-hunting Site in West Greenland. *Man and Society* 5: 5-96.
486. Gubser, N. J.
    1965 *The Nunamiut Eskimos*. Yale University Press, New Haven.
487. Guilday, J. E.
    1976 Appalachian Bone Caves. In *Geology and Biology of Pennsylvania Caves*, edited by W. B. White, pp. 88-103. Pennsylvania Geology Survey. General Geology Report, 4th Series, No. 66.
488. Guilday, J. E., P. W. Parmalee, and D. P. Tanner
    1962 Aboriginal Butchering Techniques at the Eschelman Site (36 LA 12), Lancaster County, Pennsylvania. *Pennsylvania Archaeologist* 32: 59-83.
489. Gunn, A., and F. L. Miller
    1982 Muskox Bull Killed by a Barren-Ground Grizzly Bear, Thelon Game Sanctuary, N. W. T. *Arctic* 35: 545-546.
490. Gunter, G.
    1947 Catastrophism in the Sea and Its Paleontological Significance, with Special Reference to the Gulf of Mexico. *American Journal of Science*. 245: 669-676.
491. Guthrie, R. D.
    1967 Differential Preservation and Recovery of Pleistocene Large Mammal Remains in Alaska. *Journal of Paleontology* 41: 243-246.
492. Guthrie, R. D.
    1973 Mummified Pika (Ochotona) Carcass and Dung Pellets from Pleistocene Deposits in Interior Alaska. *Journal of Mammalogy* 54: 970-971.
493. Guthrie, R. D.
    1980 The First Americans?: The Elusive Arctic Bone Culture (Review of *Pleistocene Bone Technology*, by R. Bonnichsen, 1979). *Quarterly Review of Archaeology* 1: 2.
494. Guthrie, R. D.
    1984 The Evidence for Middle-Wisconsin Peopling of Beringia: An Evaluation. *Quaternary Research* 22: 231-241.

495. Hall, S. L.
　　1984　Questions Concerning Faunal Sampling. In *Frontiers: Southern African Archaeology Today*, edited by M. Hall, G. Avery, D. M. Avery, M. L. Wilson, and A. J. B. Humphreys, pp. 373-374. British Archaeological Reports, BAR International Series No. 207. Oxford.

496. Hannus, L. A.
　　1989　Flaked Mammoth Bone from the Lange/Ferguson Site, White River Badlands Area, South Dakota. In *Bone Modification*, edited by R. Bonnichsen and M. Sorg (1st International Bone Modification Conference, Proceedings). Center for the Study of the First Americans, Orono, Maine.

497. Hanson, C. B.
　　1980　Fluvial Taphonomic Processes: Models and Experiments. In *Fossils in the Making: Vertebrate Taphonomy and Paleoecology*, edited by A. K. Behrensmeyer and A. P. Hill, pp. 156-181. University of Chicago Press, Chicago.

498. Happold, D. C. D., and M. Happold
　　1986　Small Mammals of the Zomba Plateau, as Assessed by Their Presence in Pellets of the Grass Owl, *Tyto capensis*, and by Live Trapping. *African Journal of Ecology* 24: 77-87.

499. Hare, P. E.
　　1980　Organic Geochemistry of Bone and its Relation to the Survival of Bone in the Natural Environment. In *Fossils in the Making: Vertebrate Taphonomy and Paleoecology*, edited by A. K. Behrensmeyer and A. P. Hill, pp. 208-219. University of Chicago Press, Chicago.

500. Harington, C. R.
　　1975　A Bone Tool Found with Ice Age Mammal Remains near Dawson City, Yukon Territory. *Arctic Circular* 23: 3-5.

501. Harington, C. R., R. Bonnichsen, and R. E. Morlan
　　1975　Bones Say Man Lived in the Yukon 27,000 Years Ago. *Canadian Geographical Journal* 91:42-48.

502. Harms, J. C., and R. K. Fahnestock
　　1965　Stratification, Bed Forms and Flow Phenomena (with an Example from the Rio Grande). In *Primary Sedimentary Structures and Their Hydrodynamic Interpretation*, edited by G. V. Middleton, pp. 84-115. Society of Economic Paleontologists and Mineralogists. Special Publications No. 12.

503. Harrison, T., and L. Medway
　　1962　A First Classification of Prehistoric Bone and Tooth Artifacts (Based on Material from Niah Great Cave). *Sarawak Museum Journal* 10: 335-362.

504. Hartzell, J. C.
　　1906　Conditions of Fossilization. *Journal of Geology* 14: 269-274.

505. Hay, O. P.
　　1902　*Bibliography and Catalogues of the Fossil Vertebrata of North America*. U. S. Geological Survey.

506. Hay, O. P.
　　1929 & 1930　*Second Bibliography and Catalogue of the Fossil Vertebrata of North America*. Carnegie Institute of Washington Publication, vols. 1 & 2.

507. Haynes, G. A.
　　n.d.　Evidence of Carnivore Gnawing on North American Pleistocene Mammal Bones. Ms. on file with C. P. Koch.

508. Haynes, G. A.
　　1978　Carnivore and Rodent Damage to Bone: Preliminary Statement of Experimental and Field Studies. Ms. on file with C. P. Koch.

509. Haynes, G. A.
　　1978　Excavation of Small Virginia Cave. *Archaeological Society of Virginia Quarterly Bulletin* 32: 37-41.

510. Haynes, G. A.
　　1980　Prey Bones and Predators: Potential Ecological Information from Analysis of Bone Sites. *Ossa* 7: 75-97.

511. Haynes, G. A.
　　1981　*Bone Modification and Skeletal Disturbances by Natural Agencies: Studies in North America*. Ph.D. dissertation, Catholic University of America. University Microfilms 8126907, Ann Arbor.

512. Haynes, G. A.
　　1982　Utilization and Skeletal Disturbances of North American Prey Carcasses. *Arctic* 35: 266-281.

513. Haynes, G. A.
　　1983　Frequencies of Spiral and Green-Bone Fractures on Ungulate Limb Bones in Modern Surface Assemblages. *American Antiquity* 48: 102-114.

514. Haynes, G. A.
　　1983　A Guide for Differentiating Mammalian Carnivore Taxa Responsible for Gnaw Damage to Herbivore Limb Bones. *Paleobiology* 9: 164-172.

515. Haynes, G. A.
　　1983　Review of *Bones*, by L. R. Binford. *North American Archaeologist* 4: 245-254.

516. Haynes, G. A.
　　1986　Comment on Binford and Stone 1986. *Current Anthropology* 27: 469-470.

517. Haynes, G. A., and D. Stanford
　　1984　On the possible utilization of *Camelops* by Early Man in North America. *Quaternary Research* 22: 216-230.

518. Heizer, R. F.
　　1944　Artifact Transport by Migratory Animals and Other Means. *American Antiquity* 9: 395-400.

519. Heizer, R. F.
　　1968　Migratory Animals as Dispersal Agents of Cultural Materials. *Science* 161: 914-915.

520. Henderson, P., C. A. Marlow, T. I. Molleson, and C. T. Williams
　　1983　Patterns of Chemical Change During Bone Fossilization. *Nature* 306: 358-360.

521. Hendey, Q. B., and R. Singer
　　1965　The Faunal Assemblages from the Gamtoos Valley Shelters. *South African Archaeological Bulletin* 20: 206-213.

522. Hendricks, S. B., and W. L. Hill
　　1950　The Nature of Bone and Phosphate Rock. *Geophysics* 36: 731-737.

523. Henschel, J. R., R. Tilson, and J. Von Blottnitz
    1979 Implications of a Spotted Hyaena Bone Assemblage in the Namib Desert. *South African Archaeological Bulletin* 34: 127-131.
524. Henshaw, J.
    1971 Antlers: The Unbrittle Bones of Contention. *Nature* 231: 469.
525. Herm, D.
    1972 Pitfalls in Paleoecologic Interpretation--An Integrated Approach to Avoid the Major Pits. *International Geological Congress, 24 Session, Section 7: Paleontology* pp. 82-88.
526. Herrmann, B.
    1977 On Historical Investigations of Cremated Human Remains. *Journal of Human Evolution* 6: 101-103.
527. Herrmann, G., and H. Liebowitz
    1972 Mechanics of Bone Fracture. In *Fracture*, edited by H. Liebowitz, pp. 771-840. Academic Press, New York.
528. Hewson, R.
    1984 Scavenging and Predation upon Sheep and Lambs in West Scotland. *Journal of Applied Ecology* 21: 843-868.
529. Hewson, R., and H. H. Kolb
    1976 Scavenging on Sheep Carcasses by Foxes *(Vulpes vulpes)* and Badgers *(Meles meles). Journal of Zoology* 180: 496-498.
530. Hill, A. P.
    1975 *Taphonomy of Contemporary and Late Cenozoic East African Vertebrates.* Unpublished Ph.D. dissertation, University of London, England.
531. Hill, A. P.
    1976 On Carnivore and Weathering Damage to Bone. *Current Anthropology* 17: 335-336.
532. Hill, A. P.
    1978 Taphonomical Background to Fossil Man: Problems in Palaeoecology. In *Geological Background to Fossil Man,* edited by W. W. Bishop, pp. 87-101. Scottish Academic Press, Edinburgh.
533. Hill, A. P.
    1978 Palaeoecological Significance of Bones from a Modern Hyaena Lair (Abstract). *American Journal of Physical Anthropology* 48: 405.
534. Hill, A. P.
    1978 Hyaenas, Bones and Fossil Man. *Kenya Past and Present* 9: 9-14.
535. Hill, A. P.
    1979 Butchery and Natural Disarticulation: An Investigatory Technique. *American Antiquity* 44: 739-744.
536. Hill, A. P.
    1979 Disarticulation and Scattering of Mammal Skeletons. *Paleobiology* 5: 261-274.
537. Hill, A. P.
    1980 Early Postmortem Damage to the Remains of Some East African Mammals. In *Fossils in the Making: Vertebrate Taphonomy and Paleoecology,* edited by A. K. Behrensmeyer and A. P. Hill, pp. 131-152. University of Chicago Press, Chicago.
538. Hill, A. P.
    1980 A Modern Hyaena Den in Amboseli National Park, Kenya. *Proceedings of the 8th Pan-African Congress on Prehistory and Quaternary Studies,* pp. 137-138. Nairobi.
539. Hill, A. P.
    1980 Hyena Provisioning of Juvenile Offspring at the Den. *Mammalia* 44: 594-595.
540. Hill, A. P.
    1983 Hyaenas and Early Hominids. In *Animals and Archaeology: 1. Hunters and Their Prey,* edited by J. Clutton-Brock and C. Grigson, pp. 87-92. British Archaeological Reports, BAR International Series No. 163. Oxford.
541. Hill, A. P.
    1983 Hippopotamus Butchery by *Homo erectus* at Olduvai. *Journal of Archaeological Science* 10: 135-137.
542. Hill, A. P.
    1984 Hyaenas and Hominids: Taphonomy and Hypothesis Testing. In *Hominid Evolution,* edited by R. Foley, pp. 111-128. Academic Press, London.
543. Hill, A. P.
    1989 Bone Modification by Modern Spotted Hyenas. In *Bone Modification,* edited by R. Bonnichsen and M. Sorg (1st International Bone Modification Conference, Proceedings). Center for the Study of the First Americans, Orono, Maine.
544. Hill, A. P.
    1989 Problems and Prospects of Interpreting Modified Bones from the Archaeological Record. In *Bond Modification,* edited by R. Bonnichsen and M. Sorg (1st International Bone Modification Conference, Proceedings). Center for the Study of the First Americans, Orono, Maine.
545. Hill, A. P., and A. K. Behrensmeyer
    1976 Taphonomy in East Africa: An Approach to Paleoecology. In *Palaeoecology of Africa and of the Surrounding Islands and Antartica,* vol. 9, edited by E. M. van Zinderen Bakker, pp. 123-128. A. A. Balkema, Cape Town.
546. Hill, A. P., and A. K. Behrensmeyer
    1984 Disarticulation Patterns of Some Modern East African Mammals. *Paleobiology* 10: 366-376.
547. Hill, A. P., and A. K. Behrensmeyer
    1985 Natural Disarticulation and Bison Butchery. *American Antiquity* 50: 141-145.
548. Hill, A. P., and A. C. Walker
    1972 Procedures in Vertebrate Taphonomy: Notes on a Uganda Miocene Fossil Locality. *Geological Society of London. Quarterly Journal* 128: 399-406.
549. Hillefors, A.
    1971 Deep Weathering Rock Material and Sand Grains under the Scanning Electron Microscope. *Svensk Geografisk Årsbok* 46: 138-164. Reprinted in *Lund Studies in Geography Series A. Physical Geography.* No. 49.

550. Hillman, J. C., and A. K. K. Hillman
1977 Mortality of Wildlife in Nairobi National Park, During the Drought of 1973-1974. *East African Wildlife Journal* 15: 1-18.

551. Hofman, J. L.
1986 Vertical Movement of Artifacts in Aluvial and Stratified Deposits. *Current Anthropology* 27: 163-171.

552. Hogg, G.
1966 *Cannibalism and Human Sacrifice*. The Citadel Press, New York.

553. Holtzman, R. C.
1979 Maximum Likelihood Estimation of Fossil Assemblage Composition. *Paleobiology* 5: 77-89.

554. Horton, D. R.
1984 Minimum Numbers: A Consideration. *Journal of Archaeological Science* 11: 255-271.

555. Horton, D. R., and R. V. S. Wright
1981 Cuts on Lancefield Bones; Carnivorous *Thylacoleo*, not Humans, the Cause. *Archaeology in Oceania* 16: 73-80.

556. Houston, R. S., H. Toots, and J. C. Kelly
1966 Iron Content of Fossil Bones of Tertiary Age in Wyoming Correlated with Climate Change. *Contributions to Geology* 5: 1-18.

557. Howell, F. C., G. H. Cole, and M. R. Kleindienst
1962 Isimila, an Acheulian Occupation Site in the Iringa Highlands, Southern Highlands Province, Tanganyika. In *4e Congres Pan-African du Prehistoire et de l'Etude Quaternaire, Actes*, pp. 43-80. Annales, Serie in-80: Sciences Humaines, No. 40. Musee Royale de l'Afrique Central, Tervuren, Belgium.

558. Hrdlicka, A.
1912 Early Man in South America. *U. S. Bureau of American Ethnology. Bulletin* 52: 1-9.

559. Hudson, J. D.
1978 Pyrite in Ammonite Shells and in Shales. *Neues Jahrbuch für Geologie und Paläontologie. Abhandlungen* 157: 190-193.

560. Huelke, D. F., L. J. Beuge, and J. H. Harger
1967 Bone Fractures Produced by High Velocity Impacts. *American Journal of Anatomy* 120: 123-131.

561. Hughes, A. R.
1954 Habits of Hyaenas. *South African Journal of Science* 51: 156-158.

562. Hughes, A. R.
1954 Hyenas versus Australopithecines as Agents of Bone-Accumulation. *American Journal of Physical Anthropology* 12: 467-486.

563. Hughes, A. R.
1958 Some Ancient and Recent Observations on Hyaenas. *Koedoe* 1: 105-114.

564. Hughes, A. R.
1961 Further Notes on the Habits of Hyaenas and Bone Gathering by Porcupines. *Zoological Society of Southern Africa. News Bulletin* 3: 35-37.

565. Hughes, P. J., and R. J. Lampert
1977 Occupational Disturbance and Types of Archaeological Deposits. *Journal of Archaeological Science* 4: 135-140.

566. Hunt, R. M.
1978 Depositional Setting of a Miocene Mammal Assemblage, Sioux County, Nebraska (USA). *Palaeogeography, Palaeoclimatology, Palaeoecology* 24: 1-52.

567. Hunt, R. M., X. Xiang-Xu, and J. Kaufman
1983 Miocene Burrows of Extinct Bear Dogs: Indication of Early Denning Behavior of Large Mammalian Carnivores. *Science* 221: 364-366.

568. Ikawa-Smith, F.
1985 Comment on Binford and Ho 1985 (Reply by Binford and Ho). *Current Anthropology* 26: 432.

569. Ikawa-Smith, F.
1987 Comment on Blumenschine 1987, with reply. *Current Anthropology* 28: 397.

570. Inglis, D. R.
1965 Particle Sorting and Stone Migration by Freezing and Thawing. *Science* 148: 1616-1617.

571. Inskeep, R. R., and B. Q. Hendy
1966 An Interesting Association of Bones from the Elandsfontein Fossil Site. *5e Congres Pan-African de Prehistoire et de l'Etude du Quaternaire, Actes*, pp. 109-124. Museo Arqueologico Publicaciones No. 6. Santa Cruz de Tenerife.

572. Iregren, E., and R. Jonsson
1973 Hur Ben Krymper vid Kremering. (The Shrinkage of Bones by Cremation; in Swedish). *Fornnvannen* 68: 97-100.

573. Irving, W. N., A. V. Jopling, and I. Kirtsch-Armstrong
1989 Studies of Paralithic Technology and Taphonomy, Old Crow Baisn, Yukon Territory. In *Bone Modification*, edited by R. Bonnichsen and M. Sorg (1st International Bone Modification Conference, Proceedings). Center for the Study of the First Americans, Orono, Maine.

574. Isaac, G. L.
1967 Towards the Interpretation of Occupation: Some Experiments and Observations. *Kroeber Anthropological Society. Papers* No. 37: 31-57.

575. Isaac, G. L.
1968 Traces of Pleistocene Hunters: An East African Example. In *Man the Hunter*, edited by R. B. Lee and I. DeVore, pp. 253-261. Aldine Press, Chicago.

576. Isaac, G. L.
1971 The Diet of Early Man: Aspects of Archaeological Evidence from Lower and Middle Pleistocene Sites in Africa. *World Archaeology* 2: 278-299.

577. Isaac, G. L.
1976 Researches in the Area Formerly Known as "East Rudolf": A Commentary and Classified Bibliography. In *Palaeoecology of Africa and of the Surrounding Islands and Antarctica*, vol. 9, edited by E. M. van Zinderen Bakker, pp. 109-122. A. A. Balkema, Cape Town.

578. Isaac, G. L.
1977 *Olorgesailie: Archeological Studies of a Middle Pleistocene Lake Basin in Kenya*. University of Chicago Press, Chicago.

579. Isaac, G. L.
1983 Review of *Bones*, by L. R. Binford. *American Antiquity* 48: 416-419.

580. Issac, G. L.
    1983 Bone in Contention: Competing Explanations for the Juxtaposition of Early Pleistocene Artifacts and Faunal Remains. In *Animals and Archaeology: 1. Hunters and Their Prey*, edited by J. Clutton-Brock and C. Grigson, pp. 3-19. British Archaeological Reports, BAR International Series No. 163. Oxford.
581. Issac, G. L.
    1984 Picking Bones: A Reply to Lewis Binford. (Review of *Bones*, by L. R. Binford). *American Antiquity* 49: 167-168.
582. Isaac, G. L., and D. C. Crader
    1981 To What Extent Were Early Hominids Carnivorous? An Archaeological Perspective. In *Omnivorous Primates*, edited by R. S. O. Harding and G. Teleki, pp. 37-103. Columbia University Press, New York.
583. Isaacs, W. A., K. Little, J. D. Currey, and L. B. H. Tarlo
    1963 Collagen and a Cellulose-Like Substance in Fossil Dentine and Bone. *Nature* 197: 192-194.
584. Jackes, M.
    c. 1975 The 1975 Field Season at Laetoli. Ms. on file with C. P. Koch.
585. Jackson, K. A., and D. R. Uhlmann
    1966 Particle Sorting and Stone Migration Due to Frost Heave. *Science* 152: 545-546.
586. Jacob, T.
    1972 The Problem of Head-Hunting and Brain-Eating Among Pleistocene Men in Indonesia. *Archaeology and Physical Anthropology in Oceania* 7: 81-91.
587. Jafe, E. B., and A. M. Sherwood
    1951 *Physical and Chemical Comparison of Modern and Fossil Tooth and Bone Material*. U. S. Atomic Energy Commission. TEM No. 149. Published by the U. S. Geological Survey for the Atomic Energy Commission, Technical Information Service, Oak Ridge, Tennessee.
588. Johanson, D. C., M. Splingaer, and N. T. Boaz
    1976 Paleontological Excavations in the Shungura Formation, Lower Omo Basin, 1969-1973. In *Earliest Man and Environments in the Lake Rudolf Basin*, edited by Y. Coppens, F. C. Howell, G. L. Isaac, and R. E. F. Leakey, pp. 402-420. University of Chicago Press, Chicago.
589. Johansson, C. E.
    1963 Orientation of Pebbles in Running Water: A Laboratory Study. *Geografiska Annaler* 45: 85-112.
590. Johnson, D. L., and K. L. Hansen
    1974 The Effects of Frost Heaving on Objects in Soil 1. *Plains Anthropologist* 19: 81-93.
591. Johnson, D. L., and C. V. Haynes
    1985 Camels as Taphonomic Agents. *Quaternary Research* 24: 365-366.
592. Johnson, E.
    1974 Zooarchaeology and the Lubbock Lake Site. *West Texas Museum Association. Journal* 15: 107-122.
593. Johnson, E.
    1978 Paleo-Indian Bison Procurement and Butchering Patterns on the Llano Estacado. *Plains Anthropologist* 14: 98-105.
594. Johnson, E.
    1982 Paleo-Indian Bone Expediency Tools: Lubbock Lake and Bonfire Shelter. *Canadian Journal of Anthropology* 2: 145-157.
595. Johnson, E.
    1983 A Framework for Interpretation in Bone Technology. In *Carnivores, Human Scavengers and Predators*, edited by G. M. LeMoine and A. S. MacEachern, pp. 55-93. (15th Annual Chacmool Conference, Proceedings). Archaeological Association, Department of Archaeology, University of Calgary, Alberta.
596. Johnson, E.
    1985 Current Developments in Bone Technology. Advances in Archaeological Method and Theory. In *Advances in Archaeological Method and Theory*, vol. 8, edited by M. B. Schiffer, pp. 157-235. Academic Press, New York.
597. Johnson, E.
    1989 Human Modified Bones from Early Southern Plains Sites. In *Bone Modification*, edited by R. Bonnichsen and M. Sorg (1st International Bone Modification Conference, Proceedings). Center for the Study of the First Americans, Orono, Maine.
598. Johnson, L. J., D. R. Muhs, and M. L. Barnhardt
    1977 The Effects of Frost Heaving on Objects in Soil: 2. Laboratory Experiments. *Plains Anthropologist* 22: 133-147.
599. Johnson, M. D.
    1975 Seasonal and Microseral Variations in the Insect Populations on Carrion. *American Midland Naturalist* 93: 79-90.
600. Johnson, R. G.
    1957 Experiments on the Burial of Shells. *Journal of Geology* 65: 527-535.
601. Johnson, R. G.
    1960 Models and Methods for Analysis of the Mode of Formation of Fossil Assemblages. *Geological Society of America. Bulletin* 71: 1075-1086.
602. Johnson, R. G.
    1964 The Community Approach to Paleoecology. In *Approaches to Paleoecology*, edited by J. Imbrie and N. Newell, pp. 107-134. John Wiley, New York.
603. Jones, C. M.
    1977 Effects of Varying Discharge Regimes on Bed-Form Sedimentary Structures in Modern Rivers. *Geology* 5: 567-570.
604. Jones, K. T.
    1983 Forager Archaeology: The Ache of Eastern Paraguay. In *Carnivores, Human Scavengers and Predators*, edited by G. M. LeMoine and A. S. MacEachern, pp. 171-191. (15th Annual Chacmool Conference, Proceedings). Archaeological Association, Department of Archaeology, University of Calgary, Alberta.
605. Jones, P. R.
    1980 Experimental Butchery with Modern Stone Tools and its Relevance for Palaeolithic Archaeology. *World Archaeology* 12: 153-165.
606. Jones, R., and J. Allen
    1978 Caveat Excavator: A Sea Bird Midden on Steep Head Island, North West Tasmania. *Australian Archaeology* 8: 142-145.

607. Jopling, A. V.
1965 Laboratory Study of the Distribution of Grain Size in Cross-Bedded Deposits. In *Primary Sedimentary Structures and Their Hydrodynamic Interpretation*, edited by G. V. Middleton, pp. 53-65. Society of Economic Paleontologists and Mineralogists. Special Publications No. 12.

608. Jopling, A. V.
1966 Some Principles and Techniques Used in Reconstructing the Hydraulic Parameters of a Paleo-Flow Regime. *Journal of Sedimentary Petrology* 36: 5-49.

609. Jopling, A. V.
1967 Origin of Laminae Deposited by the Movement of Ripples Along a Streambed: A Laboratory Study. *Journal of Geology* 75: 287-305.

610. Julig, P., A. V. Jopling, B. F. Beebe, J. Alcock, C. A. D'Andrea, and W. N. Irving
1983 Excavation Report on an *in situ* Bone Assemblage from Locality 12, Old Crow River, Northern Yukon. In *Carnivores, Human Scavengers and Predators*, edited by G. M. LeMoine and A. S. MacEachern, pp. 15-37. (15th Annual Chacmool Conference, Proceedings). Archaeological Association, Department of Archaeology, University of Calgary, Alberta.

611. Karega-Munene, M.
1987 *The Taphonomy of Post-Cranial Mammal Bones from Baba Jan, Iran*. Master's thesis, Department of Archaeology, University of Cambridge.

612. Karplus, H.
1972 Le Corps Humain dans la Cycle de la Nature. *Neuronio* 33:37-44.

613. Katzenburg, M.A.
1984 *Chemical Analysis of Prehistoric Human Bone from Five Temporarily Distinct Populations in Southern Ontario*. National Museum of Man, Mercury Series No. 129. Archaeological Survey of Canada, Ottawa.

614. Kauffman, E.G.
1978 Benthic Environments and Paleoecology of the Posidonienschiefer (Toarcian). *Neues Jahrbuch für Geologie und Paläontologie. Abhandlungen* 157: 18-36.

615. Keeley, H.C.M., G.E. Hudson, and J. Evans
1977 Trace Element Contents of Human Bones in Various States of Preservation: 1. The Soil Silhouette. *Journal of Archaeological Science* 4:19-24.

616. Kehoe, T.F.
1967 *The Boarding School Bison Drive Site*. Plains Anthropologist. Memoir No. 4.

617. Kehoe, T.F.
1983 Carnivores or Humans? Gull Lake Plains Hunters vs. Schreckensee German Neolithic Hunter-Farmers. In *Carnivores, Human Scavengers and Predators*, edited by G.M. LeMoine and A.S. MacEachern, pp. 157-170. (15th Annual Chacmool Conference, Proceedings). Archaeological Association, Department of Archaeology, University of Calgary, Alberta.

618. Kehoe, T.F., and A.B. Kehoe
1960 Observations on the Butchering Technique at a Prehistoric Bison-Kill in Montana. *American Antiquity* 25:420-423.

619. Keller, E.A., and W.N. Melhorn
1974 Bedforms and Fluvial Processes in Alluvial Stream Channels: Selected Observations. In *Fluvial Geomorphology*, edited by M. Morisawa, pp. 253-283. State University of New York, Binghamton.

620. Kelling, G., and P.F. Williams
1967 Flume Studies of the Reorientation of Pebbles and Shells. *Journal of Geology* 75:243-267.

621. Kent, S.
1981 The Dog: An Archaeologist's Best Friend or Worst Enemy — The Spatial Distribution of Faunal Remains. *Journal of Field Archaeology* 8:367-372.

622. Kenyon, W.A., and C.S. Churcher
1965 A Flake Tool and a Worked Antler Fragment from Late Lake Agassiz. *Canadian Journal of Earth Sciences* 2:237-246.

623. Kidwell, S.M.
1985 Models for Fossil Concentrations: Palaeobiological Implications. *Paleobiology* 12:25:31.

624. Kidwell, S.M.
1986 Palaeobiological and Sedimentological Implications of Fossil Concentrations. *Nature* 318:457-460.

625. Kidwell, S.M., and D. Jablonski
1984 Taphonomic Feedback Ecological Consequences of Shell Accumulation. In *Biotic Interactions in Recent and Fossil Benthic Communities*, edited by M.J.S. Tevesz and P.L. McCall, pp. 195-248. Plenum Press, New York.

626. Kindle, E.M.
1921 Animal Behavior as a Factor in the Formation of Bone Beds. *Canadian Field Naturalist* 25:33-34.

627. Kitching, J.W.
1963 *Bone, Tooth and Horn Tools of Palaeolithic Man: An Account of the Osteodontokeratic Discoveries in Pin Hole Cave, Derbyshire*. Manchester University Press, Manchester.

628. Kitching, J.W.
1980 On Some Fossil Arthropoda from the Limeworks, Makapansgat, Potgietersrus. *Palaeontologia Africana* 23:63-68.

629. Klein, R.G.
1975 Paleoanthropological Implications of the Nonarcheological Bone Assemblage from Swartklip 1, South-Western Cape Province, South Africa. *Quaternary Research* 5:275-288.

630. Klein, R.G.
1975 Middle Stone Age Man-Animal Relationships in Southern Africa: Evidence from Die Kelders and Klasies River Mouth. *Science* 190:265-267.

631. Klein, R.G.
1976 The Mammalian Fauna of the Klasies River Mouth Sites, Southern Cape Province, South Africa. *South African Archaeological Bulletin* 31:75-98.

632. Klein, R.G.
1977 The Mammalian Fauna from the Middle and Later Stone Age (Later Pleistocene) Levels of Border Cave, Natal Province, South Africa. *South African Archaeological Bulletin* 32:14-27.

633. Klein, R.G.
1978 The Fauna and Overall Interpretation of the "Cutting 10" Acheulean Site at Elandsfontein (Hopefield), Southwestern Cape Province, South Africa. *Quaternary Research* 10:69-83.

634. Klein, R.G.
1978 A Preliminary Report on the Larger Mammals from the Boomplaas Stone Age Site, Cango Valley, Oudtshoorn District, South Africa. *South African Archaeological Bulletin* 33:66-75.

635. Klein, R.G.
1978 Stone Age Predation on Large African Birds. *Journal of Archeological Science* 5:195-217.

636. Klein, R.G.
1980 The Interpretation of Mammalian Faunas from Stone Age Archaeological Sites with Special Reference to Sites in the Southern Big Sea Cape Province, South Africa. In *Fossils in the Making: Vertebrate Taphonomy and Paleoecology*, edited by A.K. Behrensmeyer and A.P. Hill, pp. 223-246. University of Chicago Press, Chicago.

637. Klein, R.G.
1981 Stone Age Predation on Small African Bovids. *South African Archaeological Bulletin* 36:55-65.

638. Klein, R.G.
1981 Ungulate Mortality and Sedimentary Facies in the Late Tertiary Varswater Formation, Langebaanweg, South Africa. *South African Museum. Annals* 84:233-254.

639. Klein, R.G.
1982 Patterns of Ungulate Mortality and Ungulate Mortality Profiles from Lamgebaanweg (Early Pliocene) and Elandsfontein (Middle Pleistocene) South-Western Cape Province, South Africa. *South African Museum. Annals* 90(2):49-94.

640. Klein, R.G.
1982 Bone Accumulations in Australopithecine Caves. (Review of *The Hunters or the Hunted?*, by C.K. Brain). *Paleobiology* 8:171-175.

641. Klein, R.G.
1982 Age (Mortality) Profiles as a Means of Distinguishing Hunted Species from Scavenged Ones in Stone Age Archaeological Sites. *Paleobiology* 8:151-158.

642. Klein, R.G.
1986 Comment on Bunn and Kroll 1986. *Current Anthropology* 27:446-47.

643. Klein, R.G., and K. Cruz-Uribe
1984 *Analysis of Animal Bones from Archaeological Sites*. University of Chicago Press, Chicago.

644. Koch, C.P.
1978 Modeling Taphonomic Processes in the Old Crow Basin, Yukon Territory. Paper presented at the 6th Annual Meeting of the Canadian Association of Physical Anthropologists, Niagara-on-the-Lake, Ontario.

645. Koch, C.P.
1986 *The Vertebrate Taphonomy and Palaeoecology of the Olorgesailie Formation, Middle Pleistocene, Kenya*. Ph.D. thesis, University of Toronto.

646. Koch, C.P., and R. Bonnichsen
1976 Some Methods of Inferring Hominid Activity from Vertebrate Fossil Assemblages. Paper presented at the 4th annual meeting of the Canadian Association for Physical Anthropologists, Toronto.

647. Koch, W.
1935 The Age Order of Epiphyseal Union in the Skeleton of the European Bison *(Bos bonasus* L.). *Anatomical Record* 61:371-376.

648. Konizeski, R.L.
1957 Paleoecology of the Middle Pliocene Deer Lodge Local Fauna, Western Montana. *Geological Society of America. Bulletin* 68:131-150.

649. Kontrovitz, M., S.W. Snyder, and R.J. Brown
1978 A Flume Study of the Movement of Foraminifera Tests. *Palaeogeography, Palaeoclimatology, Palaeoecology* 23:141-150.

650. Konyushkov, K.N.
1978 O Stromatolitakh kak Produktakh Zheznedeyatelnosti Iizshkh Vodoroslei (Stromatolites as Products of the Life Activity of Lower Algae; in Russian). In *Voprosy Tafonomii i Paleobiologii*, Chaired by B.S. Soklov, pp. 88-94. SSSR, Akademiya Nauk, Vsesoyuznoe Paleontologisheskoe Obshchestvo. Trudy Sessi 20. Leningrad.

651. Korschgen, L.J.
1957 Food Habits of the Coyote in Missouri. *Journal of Wildlife Management* 21:424-435.

652. Korth, W.W.
1978 *Taphonomy of Microvertebrate Fossil Assemblages*. Master's thesis, Department of Geology, University of Nebraska, Lincoln.

653. Korth, W.M.
1979 Taphonomy of Microvertebrate Assemblages. *Carnegie Museum, Pittsburgh. Annals* 48:235-285.

654. Kozlowski, J.K. (editor)
1974 *Upper Paleolithic Site with Dwellings of Mammoth Bones-Cracow, Spadzista Street B*. Folia Quaternaria No. 44.

655. Kozyar, L.A.
1978 Biotocheskie Faktory Vlkyayushchie na Zakhorohehie Spor i Pylsty v Morskikh Osadkakh i Sostav Sporo-Pylstevykh Spektrov. (Biological Factors Influencing the Burial of Spores and Pollen in Marine Sediments and the Composition of the Spore-Pollen Spectra; in Russian). In *Voprosy Tafonomii i Paleobiologii*, Chaired by B.S. Soklov, pp. 81-88. SSSR, Akademiya Nauk, Vsesoyuznoe Paleontologicheskoe Obshchestvo. Trudy Sessi 20. Leningrad.

656. Krantz, G.S.
1968 A New Method of Counting Mammal Bones. *American Journal of Archaeology* 72:286-288.

657. Kranz, P.M.
1974 The Anastrophic Burial of Bivalves and its Paleoecological Significance. *Journal of Geology* 82:237-265.

658. Kranz, P.M.
1974 Computer Simulation of Fossil Assemblage Formation Under Conditions of Anastrophic Burial. *Journal of Paleontology* 48:800-808.

659. Krejci-Graf, V.K.
    1932 Senkrechte Regelung von Schneckengehäusen. *Senckenbergiana* 14:295-299.
660. Krumbein, W.C.
    1939 Preferred Orientation of Pebbles in Sedimentary Deposits. *Journal of Geology* 47:673-706.
661. Krumbein, W.C.
    1941 The Effects of Abrasion on the Size, Shape and Roundness of Rock Fragments. *Journal of Geology* 49:482-520.
662. Krumbein, W.C.
    1942 Settling Velocity and Flume-Behavior of Non-Spherical Particles. *American Geophysical Union. Transactions* 23:621-631.
663. Krumbein, W.C., and L.L. Sloss
    1951 *Stratigraphy and Sedimentation*. W.H. Freeman, San Francisco.
664. Kruuk, H.
    1968 Hyenas: The Hunters Nobody Knows. *National Geographic Magazine* 134:44-57.
665. Kruuk, H.
    1972 *The Spotted Hyena: A Study of Predation and Social Behavior*. University of Chicago Press, Chicago.
666. Kruuk, H.
    1976 Social Behavior and Foraging of the Striped Hyaena (*Hyaena vulgaris*). *East African Wildlife Journal* 14:91-111.
667. Kruuk, H., and M. Turner
    1967 Comparative Notes on Predation by Lion, Leopard, Cheetah and Wild Dog in the Serengeti Area, East Africa. *Mammalia* 31:1-27.
668. Kuenen, P.H.
    1955 Experimental Abrasion of Pebbles: 1. Wet Sandblasting. *Leidse Geologische Mededelingen* 20:142-147.
669. Kuenen, P.H.
    1956 Experimental Abrasion of Pebbles: 2. Rolling by Current. *Journal of Geology* 64:336-368.
670. Kuenen, P.H.
    1959 Experimental Abrasion: 3. Fluviatile Action on Sand. *American Journal of Science* 257:172-190.
671. Kuenen, P.H.
    1960 Experimental Abrasion: 4. Eolian Action. *Journal of Geology* 68:427-449.
672. Kuenen, P.H.
    1962 Experimental Abrasion: 5. Frosting and Defrosting of Quartz Grains. *Journal of Geology* 70:648-658.
673. Kühne, W.G.
    1956 *The Liassic Therapsid Oligokyphus*. British Museum (Natural History), London.
674. Kulikov, M.V., and L.I. Khozatskiy
    1978 I.A. Efremov: Osnovatel Tafonomii (I.A. Efremov: The Founder of Taphonomy; in Russian). In *Voprosy Tafonomii i Paleobiologii*, Chaired by B.S. Soklov, pp. 17-38. SSSR, Akademiya Nauk, Vsesoyuznoe Paleontologicheskoe Obshchestvo. Trudy Sessi 20. Leningrad.
675. Kusmer, K.
    1985 Owl pellet taphonomy: Archaeological Considerations. Paper presented at the 18th Annual Meeting of the Canadian Archaeological Association, Winnipeg.
676. Kuss, S.E.
    1969 Die Paläolithische Osteokeratische Kultur der Insel Kreta (Griechenland) (English abstract). *Naturforschende Gesellschaft, Freiburg im Breisgau. Bericht* 59:137-168.
677. LaBarbera, M.
    1977 Brachiopod Orientation to Water Movement: 1. Theory, Laboratory Behavior, and Field Orientations. *Paleobiology* 3:270-287.
678. Lafont, R., and N. Petit-Maire
    1978 Les Acides Aminées du Collagène: Perspectives d'Étude d'Ossements Humains Fossiles. *Société d'Anthropologie de Paris, Bulletins et Mémoirs*. Séries 13, 5:139-142.
679. Lakes, R., and S. Saha
    1979 Cement Line Motion in Bone. *Science* 204:501-503.
680. Lambert, J.B., S.V. Simpson, C.B. Szpunar, and J.E. Buikstra
    1985 Bone Diagenesis and Dietary Analysis. *Journal of Archaeological Science* 14:477-482.
681. Lanata, J.L.
    1985 Comment on Binford and Ho 1985 (Reply by Binford and Ho). *Current Anthropology* 26:432.
682. Langbein, W.B., and L.B. Leopold
    1968 *River Channel Bars and Dunes: Theory of Kinematic Waves*. U.S. Geological Survey. Professional Paper 422-L.
683. Laporte, L.F., and A.K. Behrensmeyer
    1980 Tracks and Substrate Reworking by Terrestrial Vertebrates in Quaternary Sediments of Kenya. *Journal of Sedimentary Petrology* 50:1337-1346.
684. Larson, D.W.
    1977 Differential Shell Burial and Transport as a Function of Morphology: Potential to Bias the Geologic Record. *Geological Society of America. Abstracts with Programs* 9:620.
685. Lasker, H.
    1976 Effects of Differential Preservation on the Measurement of Taxonomic Diversity. *Paleobiology* 2:84-93.
686. Lawrence, D.R.
    1968 Taphonomy and Information Loss in Fossil Communities. *Geological Society of America. Bulletin* 79:1315-1330.
687. Lawrence, D.R.
    1971 The Nature and Structure of Paleoecology. *Journal of Paleontology* 45:593-607.
688. Lawton, R.C.
    1976 *Taphonomy and Paleohydraulics: Morrison Formation, Northwestern Utah*. Senior thesis, University of California, Santa Cruz.
689. Lawton, R.C.
    1977 Taphonomy of the Dinosaur Quarry, Dinosaur National Monument. *Contributions to Geology* 15:119-126.

690. Leakey, L.S.B.
1968 Bone Smashing by Late Miocene Hominidae. *Nature* 218:528-530.

691. Leakey, M.D.
1971 *Olduvai Gorge*, vol. 3. Cambridge University Press, Cambridge.

692. Leechman, D.
1951 Bone Grease. *American Antiquity* 16:355-356.

693. LeMort, F.
1981 *Degradations Artificielles sur des Os Humains de Paléolithique*. Diploma du Docteur 2e Cycle Thesis, L'Université Pierre et Marie Curie, Paris.

694. Leopold, L.B.
1951 Rainfall Frequency: An Aspect of Climatic Variation. *American Geophysical Union. Transactions* 32:347-357.

695. Leopold, L.B.
1974 *Water: A Primer*. W.H. Freeman, San Francisco.

696. Leopold, L.B.
1976 Reversal of Erosion Cycle and Climate Change. *Quaternary Research* 6:557-562.

697. Leopold, L.B., M.G. Wolman, and J.P. Miller
1964 *Fluvial Processes in Geomorphology*. W.H. Freeman, San Francisco.

698. Leopold, L.B., W.W. Emmett, and R.M. Myrick
1966 *Channel and Hillslope Processes in a Semi-Arid Area, New Mexico*. U.S. Geological Survey. Professional Paper No. 352-G.

699. Leroi-Gourhan, A., and M. Brézillon
1972 *Fouilles de Pincevent, Essai d'Analyse Ethnographique d'un Habitat Magdalénien*. (La Section 36). Centre National de la Recherche Scientifique, Paris. (7. Supplement a Gallia Prehistoire).

700. Lever, J.
1958 Quantitative Beach Research: 1. The "Left-Right Phenomenon": Sorting of Lamellibranch Valves on Sandy Beaches. *Basteria* 22:21-51.

701. Lever, J., A. Kessler, A.P. van Overbeeks, and R. Thijssen
1961 Quantitative Beach Research: 2. The Hole Effect: A Second Mode of Sorting of Lamellibranch Valves on Sandy Beaches. *Netherlands Journal of Sea Research* 1:339-358.

702. Lever, J., M. van den Bosch, H. Cook, T. van Dijk, A.J.H. Thiadens, and R. Thijssen
1964 Quantitative Beach Research: 3. An Experiment with Artificial Valves of *Donax vittatus*. *Netherlands Journal of Sea Research* 2:458-492.

703. Levine, M.A.
1983 Review of: *Bison Kills and Bone Counts: Decision Making by Ancient Hunters*, by J.D. Speth. *Journal of Archaeological Science* 10:554-555.

704. Levinson, M.
1982 Taphonomy of Microvertebrates: From Owl Pellets to Cave Breccia. *Transvaal Museum, Pretoria. Annals* 33:115-121.

705. Lewin, R.
1983 Archaeological Analysis Gets Some Teeth. (Review of *Analysis of Animal Bones from Archaeological sites*, by R.G. Klein and K. Cruz-Uribe). *Science* 221:446-447.

706. Lewy, Z.
1981 Maceration of Calcareous Skeletons. *Sedimentology* 28:893-895.

707. Lighthill, J.J., and G.B. Whitham
1955 On Kinematic Waves: 1. Flood Movement in Long Rivers. *Royal Society of London. Proceedings* 229A:281-316.

708. Lighthill, J.J., and G.B. Whitham
1955 On Kinematic Waves: 2. A Theory of Traffic Flow on Long Crowded Roads. *Royal Society of London. Proceedings* 229A:317-345.

709. Lisowski, F.P.
1968 The Investigation of Human Cremations. In *Anthropologie und Humangenetik*, pp. 76-83. G. Fischer, Stuttgart.

710. Lisowski, F.P.
1979 Human Remains from Shun Wan, Hong Kong, with Observation of the Practice of Cremation in Ancient China. *Homo* 30:95-106.

711. Loomis, F.B.
1910 The Genus Stenomylus: Osteology and Affinities of the Genus Stenomylus. *American Journal of Science* 29:297-323.

712. Long, C.A., and W.C. Kerfoot
1963 Mammalian Remains from Owl-pellets in Eastern Wyoming. *Journal of Mammalogy* 44:129-131.

713. Losey, T.C.
1971 Notes on Athapaskan Butchering Techniques No. 1. *Archaeological Society of Alberta. Newsletter* 26:1-6.

714. Lü, Z.
1985 Comment on Binford and Ho 1985 (Reply by Binford and Ho). *Current Anthropology* 26:432-433.

715. Luchterhand, K.
1985 Comment on Binford and Ho 1985 (Reply by Binford and Ho). *Current Anthropology* 26:432-434.

716. Lundelius, E.L.
1960 Post Pleistocene Faunal Succession in Western Australia and its Climatic Interpretation. *International Geological Congress, 21st Report* 4:142-153.

717. Lundelius, E.L.
1963 Vertebrate Remains from the Nullarbor Caves, Western Australia. *Royal Society of Western Australia. Journal* 46:75-80.

718. Lupton, C.
1979 Taphonomy of a Late Cretaceous Vertebrate Fossil Locality, McCone County, Montana (Abstract). *Geological Society of America. Program with Abstracts* 11(5):234-235.

719. Lupton, C., D. Gabriel, and R.M. West
1980 Paleobiology and Depositional Setting of a Late Cretaceous Vertebrate Locality, Hell Creek Formation, McCone County, Montana. *Contributions to Geology* 18:117-126.

720. Lyman, R.L.
1977 Analysis of Historic Faunal Remains. *Historical Archaeology* 11:67-73.

721. Lyman, R.L.
1978 Formation of the Archaeofaunal Record: A Preliminary Model. Paper presented at the 31st Annual Northwest Anthropology Conference, Pullman.

722. Lyman, R.L.
1978 Prehistoric Butchering Techniques in the Lower Granite Reservoir, Southeastern Washington. *Tebiwa* 13:1-25.

723. Lyman, R.L.
1979 *Archaeological Faunal Analysis: A Bibliography*. Idaho Museum of Natural History, Occasional Paper No. 31.

724. Lyman, R.L.
1979 Available Meat from Faunal Remains: A Consideration of Techniques. *American Antiquity* 44:536-546.

725. Lyman, R.L.
1979 Faunal Analysis: An Outline of Method and Theory with Some Suggestions. *Northwest Anthropological Research Notes* 13:22-35.

726. Lyman, R.L.
1980 Inferences from Bone Distribution in Prehistoric Sites in the Lower Granite Reservoir Area, Southeastern Washington. *Northwest Anthropological Research Notes* 14:107-123.

727. Lyman, R.L.
1982 *The Taphonomy of Archaeofaunas: Bone Density and Differential Survivorship of Fossil Classes*. Ph.D. dissertation, University of Washington, University Microfilms 8218245, Ann Arbor.

728. Lyman, R.L.
1982 Archaeofaunas and Subsistence Studies. In *Advances in Archaeological Method and Theory*, vol. 5, edited by M.B. Schiffer, pp. 331-393. Academic Press, New York.

729. Lyman, R.L.
1984 Bone Density and Differential Survivorship of Fossil Classes. *Journal of Anthropological Archaeology* 3:259-299.

730. Lyman, R.L.
1984 Broken Bones, Bone Expediency Tools, and Bone Pseudotools: Lessons from the Blast Zone Around Mount St. Helens, Washington. *American Antiquity* 49:315-333.

731. Lyman, R.L.
1985 Comment on Binford and Ho 1985 (Reply by Binford and Ho). *Current Anthropology* 26:434.

732. Lyman, R.L.
1987 Hunting for Evidence of Plio-Pleistocene Hominid Scavengers (Comment on Shipman 1986, with reply by Shipman). *American Anthropologist* 89:710-717.

733. Lyman, R.L.
1987 Archaeofaunas and Butchery Studies: A Taphonomic Perspective. In *Advances in Archaeological Method and Theory*, vol. 10, edited by M.B. Schiffer, pp. 249-337. Academic Press, New York.

734. Lyman, R.L.
1987 Bone Frequencies: Differential Transport, *In situ* Destruction, and the MGUI. *Journal of Archaeological Science* 12:221-236.

735. Lyman, R.L.
1987 Zooarchaeology and Taphonomy: A General Consideration. *Journal of Ethnobiology* 7:93-117.

736. Lyman, R.L.
1989 Taphonomy of Cervids Killed by the 18 May 1980 Volcanic Eruptions of Mount St. Helens. In *Bone Modification*, edited by R. Bonnichsen and M. Sorg (1st International Bone Modification Conference, Proceedings). Center for the Study of the First Americans, Orono, Maine, in press.

737. Lyman, R.L., and M.J. O'Brien
1978 Plow-zone Zooarchaeology: Fragmentation and Indentifiability. *Journal of Field Archaeology* 14:493-498.

738. Lyon, P.J.
1970 Differential Bone Destruction: An Ethnographic Example. *American Antiquity* 35:213-215.

739. Lyuleva, S.A.
1978 Ekologicheskie Faktory Formirobaniya i Tafonomiya Izvestkovogo Nanoplanktona (Ecological Factors of the Formation and Taphonomy of Calcareous Nanoplankton; in Russian). In *Voprosy Tafonomii i Paleobiologii*, Chaired by B.S. Soklov, pp. 158-165. SSSR, Akademiya Nauk, Vsesoyuznoe Paleontologicheskoe Obshchestvo. Trudy Sessi 20. Leningrad.

740. MacDonald, D.W.
1978 Observations on the Behavior and Ecology of the Striped Hyaena *(Hyaena hyaena)* in Israel. *Israel Journal of Zoology* 27(4):189-198.

741. MacDonald, D.W.
1983 The Ecology of Carnivore Social Behaviour. *Nature* 301:379-384.

742. MacDonald, K.B.
1976 Paleocommunities: Toward Some Confidence Limits. In *Structure and Classification of Paleocommunities*, edited by R.W. Scott and R.R. West, pp. 87-106. Dowden, Hutchinson and Ross, Stroudsburg, PA.

743. MacGregor, A.G.
1975 Problems in the Interpretation of Microscopic Wear Patterns: The Evidence from Bone Skates. *Journal of Archaeological Science* 2:385-390.

744. MacGregor, A.G.
1985 *Bone, Antler, Ivory and Horn: The Technology of Skeletal Materials Since the Roman Period*. Barnes and Noble, Totowa, New Jersey.

745. MacGregor, A.G., and J.D. Curry
1983 Mechanical Properties as Conditioning Factors in the Bone and Antler Industry of the 3rd to the 13th Century A.D. *Journal of Archaeological Science* 10:71-77.

746. Maguire, J.M., D. Pemberton, and M.H. Collett
1980 The Makapansgat Limeworks Grey Breccia: Hominids, Hyaenas, Hystricids or Hillwash. *Palaeontologia Africana* 23:75-98.

747. Maiklem, W.R.
1968 Some Hydraulic Properties of Bioclastic Carbonate Grains. *Sedimentology* 10:101-109.

748. Maltby, J.M.
1985 Patterns of Faunal Assemblage Variability. In *Beyond Domestication in Prehistoric Europe*, edited by G. Baker and C. Gamble, pp. 33-74. Academic Press, London.

749. Marean, C.W.
    1987 Comment on Blumenschine 1987, with reply. *Current Anthropology* 28:397-398.
750. Marker, M.E., and T.M. Evers
    1976 Iron Age Settlement and Soil Erosion in the Eastern Transvaal, South Africa. *South African Archaeological Bulletin* 31:153-165.
751. Marshall, F.B.
    1986 *Aspects of the Advent of Pastoral Economies in East Africa*. Ph.D. dissertation, University of California, Berkeley. University Microfilms DA8624854, Ann Arbor.
752. Marshall, F.B.
    1986 Implications of Bone Modification in a Neolithic Faunal Assemblage for the Study of Early Hominid Butchery and Subsistence Practices. *Journal of Human Evolution* 15:661-672.
753. Marshall, L.
    1989 Bone Modification and "The Laws of Burial." In *Bone Modification*, edited by R. Bonnichsen and M. Sorg (1st International Bone Modification Conference, Proceedings). Center for the Study of the First Americans, Orono, Maine.
754. Martin, H.
    1910 La Percussion Osseuse et les Esquilles qui en Dérivent Expérimentation. *Société Préhistorique Française Bulletin* 7:299-309.
755. Martin, R.
    1960 Principles of Paleogeomorphology. *Canadian Mining and Metallurgical Bulletin* 53:529-538.
756. Martinell, J., R. Domenech, and M.J. Marquina
    1980 Premisas para el Analisis Paleontologico. *Sociedad Española de Historia Natural, Boletín de la Secciín Geológica* 78:133-140.
757. Martinka, C.J.
    1969 An Incidence of Mass Elk Drowning. *Journal of Mammalogy* 50:640-641.
758. Mason, R.J.
    1961 The Earliest Tool-Makers in South Africa. *South African Journal of Science* 57:13-16.
759. Mason, R.J., R.A. Dart, and J.W. Kitching
    1958 Bone Tools at the Kalkbank Middle Stone Age Site and the Makapansgat Australopithicus Locality, Central Transvaal. *South African Archaeological Bulletin* 13:105-116.
760. Matthews, J.M.
    1965 Stratigraphic Disturbance: The Human Element. *Antiquity* 39:295-298.
761. Mayhew, D.F.
    1977 Avian Predators as Accumulators of Fossil Mammal Material. *Boreas* 6:25-31.
762. Mbae, B.N.
    1986 *Aspects of Maasai Ethnoarchaeology: Implications for Archaeological Interpretations*. Master's thesis, Department of History, University of Nairobi.
763. McArdle, J.E.
    1974 *A Numerical (Computerized) Method for Quantifying Zooarchaeological Comparisons*. Master's thesis, Department of Geological Sciences, University of Illinois, Chicago.
764. McArdle, J.E.
    1976/77 A Numerical (Computerized) Method for Quantifying Zooarcheological Comparisons. *Paleorient* 3:181-190.
765. McCarthy, B.
    1977 Selective Preservation of Molluscan Shells in a Permian Beach Environment, Sydney Basin, Australia. *Neues Jarbuch für Geologie und Paläeontologie Monatsefte.* 1977:466-474.
766. McCormick, J.S.
    1982 Establishing Criteria in Archaeological Faunal Analysis. *Canadian Journal of Anthropology* 2:179-188.
767. McCullough, K.M.
    1978 *Modified Deer Phalanges at the Draper Site*. Museum of Indian Archaeology, London, Ontario. Research Report No. 5.
768. McGrew, P.O.
    1963 Environmental Significance of Sharks in the Shotgun Fauna, Paleocene of Wyoming. *Contribution to Geology* 2:39-41.
769. McGrew, P.O.
    1975 Taphonomy of Eocene Fish from Fossil Basin, Wyoming. *Fieldiana. Geology* 33:257-270.
770. McHenry, H.M., and C.J. O'Brien
    1986 Comment on Bunn and Kroll 1986. *Current Anthropology* 27:447.
771. McKee, E.D.
    1964 Inorganic Sedimentary Structures. In *Approaches to Paleoecology*, edited by J. Imbrie and N. Newell, pp. 275-295. John Wiley, New York.
772. McKnight, D.G.
    1969 A Recent Possible Catastrophic Burial in a Marine Molluscan Community. *New Zealand Journal of Marine and Freshwater Resources* 3:177-179.
773. McLean, F.C., and M.R. Urist
    1961 *Bone*. 2nd ed. University of Chicago Press, Chicago.
774. Mead, E., and S. Meeks
    1989 Photography of Archaeological and Paleontological Bone Specimens. In *Bone Modification*, edited by R. Bonnichsen and M. Sorg (1st International Bone Modification Conference, Proceedings). Center for the Study of the First Americans, Orono, Maine.
775. Meadow, R.H.
    1978 "BONECODE"—A System of Numerical Coding for Faunal Data from Middle Eastern Sites. *Peabody Museum of Archaeology and Ethnology. Bulletin* 2:169-186.
776. Mech, L.D.
    1970 *The Wolf: The Ecology and Behavior of an Endangered Species*. Natural History Press, New York.
777. Mellett, J.S.
    1974 Scatological Origin of Microvertebrate Fossil Accumulations. *Science* 185:349-350.
778. Menard, H.W., and A.J. Boucot
    1951 Experiments on the Movement of Shells by Water. *American Journal of Science* 249:131-151.

779. Mengoni Goñalons, G.
   1985 Comment on Binford and Ho 1985 (Reply by Binford and Ho). *Current Anthropology* 26:434-435.
780. Mercier, M.L.
   1935 La Pointe en Os a Cran de l'Aurignacien Inferieur. *Compte Rendu 11th Congres Prehistorique de France*, pp. 119-120. Périgueux.
781. Merriam, J.C.
   1906 Recent Cave Exploration in California. *American Anthropologist* 8:221-228.
782. Middleton, G.V. (editor)
   1965 *Primary Sedimentary Structures and Their Hydrodynamic Interpretations*. Society of Economic Paleontologists and Mineralogists. Special Publications No. 12.
783. Miller, G.J.
   1969 A Study of Cuts, Grooves, and Other Marks on Recent and Fossil Bone: 1. Animal Tooth Marks. *Tebiwa* 12:20-26.
784. Miller, G.J.
   1975 A Study of Cuts, Grooves, and Other Marks on Recent and Fossil Bone: 2. Weathering Cracks, Fractures, Splinters, and Other Similar Natural Phenomena. In *Lithic Technology*, edited by E. Swanson, pp. 211-226. Mouton, The Hague.
785. Miller, G.S.
   1940 Bones of Mammals Collected by Baird in Pennsylvania Caves. *Journal of Mammalogy* 21:319-322.
786. Miller, J.E.
   1984 *Basic Concepts of Kinematic Wave Models*. U.S. Geological Survey. Professional Paper 1302.
787. Miller, M.C., I.N. McCave, and P.D. Komar
   1977 Threshold of Sediment Motion Under Unidirectional Currents. *Sedimentology* 24:507-527.
788. Miller, S.J.
   1977 Osteo-Archaeology of the Mammoth-Bison Assemblage at Owl Cave, the Wasden Site, Idaho: Preliminary Report. Paper presented at the annual meeting of the Society for American Archaeology, New Orleans.
789. Miller, S.J.
   1983 Osteo-Archaeology of the Mammoth-Bison Assemblage at Owl Cave, the Wasden Site, Idaho. In *Carnivores, Human Scavengers and Predators*, edited by G.M. LeMoine and A.S. MacEachern, pp. 39-53. (15th Annual Chacmool Conference, Proceedings). Archaeological Association, Department of Archaeology, University of Calgary, Alberta.
790. Miller, W., and L.A. Alvis
   1986 Temporal Change as an Aspect of Biogenic Shell Utilization and Damage, Pleistocene of North Carolina, U.S.A. *Palaeogeography, Palaeoclimatology, Palaeoecology* 56:197-215.
791. Miller, S.J.
   1989 Characteristics of Mammoth Bone Reduction at Owl Cave, the Wasden Site, Idaho. In *Bone Modification*, edited by R. Bonnichsen and M. Sorg (1st International Bone Modification Conference, Proceedings). Center for the Study of the First Americans, Orono, Maine, in press.

792. Mills, M.G.L.
   1978 Foraging Behaviour of the Brown Hyaena (*Hyaena brunnea* Thunberg, 1820) in the Southern Kalahari. *Zeitschrift fur Tierpsychologie* 48:113-141.
793. Mills, M.G.L., and M.E.J. Mills
   1977 An Analysis of Bones Collected at Hyaena Breeding Dens in the Gemsbok National Parks. *Transvaal Museum, Pretoria. Annals* 30:145-159.
794. Minikh, M.G.
   1978 K Tafonomii Dvoyakodyshashchikh Ryb v Triase Vostoka Evropeiskoi Chasti SSSR (The Taphonomy of Dipnoi Fish in the Triassic of the Russian Platform; in Russian). In *Voprosy Tafonomii i Paleobiologii*, Chaired by B.S. Soklov, pp. 94-100. SSSR, Akademiya Nauk, Vsesoyuznoe Paleontologicheskoe Obshchestvo. Trudy Sessi 20. Leningrad.
795. Minnegal, M.M.A.
   1982 *Dugong Processing as an Archaeological Phenomenon: Evidence from a Small Complex of Sites at Princess Charlotte Bay, North Queensland*. B.A. thesis, University of Queensland, Brisbane.
796. Minnegal, M.M.A.
   1984 Dugong Bones from Princess Charlotte Bay. *Australian Archaeology* 18:63-71.
797. Miyadi, D., and T. Habe
   1947 On Thanatocoenoses of Bays (in Japanese, English summary). *Seiri Seital (Physiology and Ecology)* 1:110-124.
798. Moeyersons, J.
   1978 The Behavior of Stones and Implements, Buried in Consolidating and Creeping Kalahari Sands. *Earth Surface Processes* 3:115-128.
799. Mohl, U.
   1972 Animal Bones from Itivnera, West Greenland. *Meddelelser Om Grönland* 191(6):3-23.
800. Montgomery, T.H., Jr.
   1899 Observations on Owls, with Particular Regard to Their Feeding Habits. *American Naturalist* 33:563-572.
801. Moon, E.L.
   1940 Notes on Hawk and Owl Pellet Formation and Identification. *Kansas Academy of Science. Transactions* 43:457-466.
802. Morlan, R.E.
   1978 Early Man in Northern Yukon Territory: Perspectives as of 1977. In *Early Man in America from a Circumpacific Perspective*, edited by A.L. Bryan, pp. 78-95. University of Alberta, Department of Anthropology. Occasional Papers No. 1.
803. Morlan, R.E.
   1980 *Taphonomy and Archaeology in the Upper Pleistocene of the Northern Yukon Territory: A Glimpse of the Peopling of the New World*. Archaeological Survey of Canada, Paper No. 94. Mercury Series, National Museum of Man, Ottawa.

804. Morlan, R.E.
    1983 Spiral Fractures on Limb Bones: Which Ones are Artificial? In *Carnivores, Human Scavengers and Predators*, edited by G.M. LeMoine and A.S. MacEachern, pp. 241-269. (15th Annual Chacmool Conference, Proceedings). Archaeological Association, Department of Archaeology, University of Calgary, Calgary, Alberta.

805. Morlan, R.E.
    1983 Counts and Estimates of Taxonomic Abundance in Faunal Remains: Microtine Rodents from Bluefish Cave I. *Canadian Journal of Archaeology* 7:61-76.

806. Morlan, R.E.
    1984 Toward the Definition of Criteria for the Recognition of Artifical Bone Alterations. *Quaternary Research* 22:160-171.

807. Morlan, R.E.
    1986 Review of *Bison Kills and Bone Counts* by J.D. Speth. *American Antiquity* 51:196-197.

808. Morlan, R.E., and R. Bonnichsen
    1975 Early Human Occupations in Old Crow Flats, Yukon: The Nature of the Evidence. Paper presented at the Symposium on Correlation of the Ancient Cultures of Siberia and Adjoining Territories of the Pacific Coast, Novosibirsk.

809. Morlan, R.E., and J.V. Matthews
    1983 Taphonomy and Paleoecology of Fossil Insect Assemblages from Old Crow (CR H-15), Northern Yukon Territory, Canada. *Geographie Physique et Quaternaire* 37:147-157.

810. Moskina, O.D., and V.M. Matsuy
    1978 Tafonomiya Osnovnykh Zaknoronenii Melkikh Mlekopitayushchikh Pozdnego Kainozoya Vostochnogo Kazakhstana (The Taphonomy of the Basic Burial of Small Mammals of the Upper Cenozoic in Eastern Kazakhstan; in Russian). In *Voprosy Tafonomii i Paleobiologii*, Chaired by B.S. Soklov, pp. 100-108. SSSR, Akademiya Nauk, Vesoyuznoe Paleontologicheskoe Obshchestvo. Trudy Sessi 20. Leningrad.

811. Moss, C.
    1975 The Ugly Hyena Turns Out to be a Superb Predator. *Smithsonian* 6(3):38-54.

812. Mott, N.F.
    1947 Fragmentation of Shell Cases. *Royal Society of London. Proceedings, Series A* 189:300-308.

813. Müller, A.H.
    1950 Grundlagen der Biostratonomie. *Deutschen Akademie der Wissenschaften. Klasse fur Mathematik und Allgemeine Naturwissenschaften. Abhandlungen* 3:1-146.

814. Mundy, P.J., and J.A. Ledger
    1976 Griffon Vultures, Carnivores and Bones. *South African Journal of Science* 72:106-110.

815. Munthe, K., and S.A. McLeod
    1975 Collection of Taphonomic Information from Fossil and Recent Vertebrate Specimens with a Selected Bibiography. *PaleoBios* 19:1-12.

816. Murie, O.J.
    1946 Evaluating Duplications in Analyses of Coyote Scats. *Journal of Wildlife Management* 10:275-276.

817. Myers, T.P., M.R. Voorhies, and G. Corner
    1980 Spiral Fractures and Bone Pseudotools at Paleontological Sites. *American Antiquity* 45:483-490.

818. Nagle, J.S.
    1964 Differential Sorting of Shells in the Swash Zone (Abstract). *Biological Bulletin* 127:353.

819. Nagle, J.S.
    1964 Wave and Current Orientation of Shells (Abstract). *Geological Society of America. Special Paper* No. 82.

820. Nagle, J.S.
    1967 Wave and Current Orientation of Shells. *Journal of Sedimentary Petrology* 37:1124-1138.

821. Nelson, N.C.
    1928 Pseudo-Artifacts from the Pliocene of Nebraska. *Science* 67:316-317.

822. Neugebauer, J.
    1978 Echinodermen-Diageneses. *Neues Jahrbuch für Geologie und Paläontologie. Abhandlungen* 157:193-195.

823. Neumann, T.W.
    1978 A Model for the Vertical Distribution of Flotation-Size Particles. *Plains Anthropologist* 23:85-101.

824. Newcomer, M.H.
    1974 Study and Replication of Bone Tools from Ksar Akil (Lebanon). *World Archaeology* 6:138-153.

825. Newell, N.D.
    1959 The Nature of the Fossil Record. *American Philosophical Society. Proceedings* 103:264-285.

826. Nickens, P.R.
    1975 Prehistoric Cannibalism in the Mancos Canyon, Southwestern Colorado. *Kiva* 40:283-293.

827. Noble, J.P.A., and A. Logan
    1981 Size-Frequency Distributions and Taphonomy of Brachipods: A Recent Model. *Palaeogeography, Palaeoclimatology, Palaeoecology* 36:87-105.

828. Noe-Nygaard, N.
    1971 Spur Dog Spines from Prehistoric and Early Historic Denmark. *Dansk Geologisk Forening. Bulletin* (Geological Society of Denmark. Bulletin) 21:18-33.

829. Noe-Nygaard, N.
    1973 New Interpretation of Shoulder-Blade Scrapers. *Dansk Geologisk Forening. Bulletin* (Geological Society of Denmark. Bulletin) 22:249-253.

830. Noe-Nygaard, N.
    1973 The Vig Bull: New Information on the Final Hunt. *Dansk Geologisk Forening. Bulletin* (Geological Society of Denmark. Bulletin) 22:244-248.

831. Noe-Nygaard, N.
    1974 Mesolithic Hunting in Denmark Illustrated by Bone Injuries Caused by Human Weapons. *Journal of Archaeological Science* 1:217-248.

832. Noe-Nygaard, N.
    1975 Bone Injuries Caused by Human Weapons in Mesolithic Denmark. In *Archaeozoological Studies*, edited by A.T. Clason, pp. 151-159. American Elsevier, New York.

833. Noe-Nygaard, N.
   1975 Two Shoulder Blades with Healed Lesions from Starr Carr. *Prehistoric Society (Denmark). Proceedings* 41:10-16.

834. Noe-Nygaard, N.
   1975 *Taphonomy in Archaeology with Special Emphasis on the Role of Marrow Fracturing.* Unpublished Ph.D. dissertation, Department of History, Geology and Paleontology, University of Copenhagen, Denmark.

835. Noe-Nygaard, N.
   1977 Butchering and Marrow Fracturing as a Taphonomic Factor in Archaeological Deposits. *Paleobiology* 3:218-237.

836. North, M.E.W.
   1948 The Lammergeyer in Kenya Colony. *Ibis* 90:138-141.

837. Novak, I.D.
   1973 Predicting Coarse Sediment Transport: The Hjulstrom Curve Revisited. In *Fluvial Geomorphology*, edited by M. Morisawa, pp.13-25. State University of New York, Binghamton.

838. Nye, P.H.
   1955 Some Soil-Forming Processes in the Humid Tropics: 4. The Action of the Soil Fauna. *Journal of Soil Sciences* 6:73-83.

839. Oakley, K.P.
   1957 *Man the Tool-Maker.* University of Chicago Press, Chicago.

840. Octobon, E., C. Begouen, and L. Begouen
   1935 Outillages en Os du Paléolithique Supérieur. *Compte Rendu 11th Congrès Préhistorique de France*, pp. 186-188. Périgueux.

841. Oldham, C.
   1930 The Shell-smashing Habit of Gulls. *Ibis* 6:239-243.

842. Oliver, J.S.
   1989 Analogues and Site Context: Bone Damages from Shield Trap Cave (24CB91), Carbon County, Montana. In *Bone Modification*, edited by R. Bonnichsen and M. Sorg (1st International Bone Modification Conference, Proceedings). Center for the Study of the First Americans, Orono, Maine.

843. Olsen, J.W.
   1986 Comment on Binford and Stone 1986. *Current Anthropology* 27:470-71.

844. Olsen, S.J.
   1961 The Relative Value of Fragmentary Mammalian Remains. *American Antiquity* 26:538-540.

845. Olsen, S.J.
   1971 *Zooarchaeology: Animal Bones in Archaeology and Their Interpretation.* Addison-Wesley, Reading, Massachusetts.

846. Olson, E.C.
   1957 Size-Frequency Distributions in Samples of Extinct Organisms. *Journal of Geology* 65:309-333.

847. Olson, E.C.
   1962 Late Permian Terrestrial Vertebrates, USA and USSR. *American Philosophical Society, Transactions* 52(pt. 2).

848. Olson, E.C.
   1980 Taphonomy: Its History and Role in Community Evolution. In *Fossils in the Making: Vertebrate Taphonomy and Paleoecology*, edited by A.K. Behrensmeyer and A.P. Hill, pp. 5-19. University of Chicago Press, Chicago.

849. Olson, E.C.
   1985 Vertebrate Paleoecology: A Current Perspective. *Palaeogeography, Palaeoclimatology, Palaeoecology* 50:83-106.

850. Osgood, C.
   1936 *Contributions to the Ethnography of the Kutchin.* Yale University Publications in Anthropology No. 14. New Haven.

851. Oshurkova, M.V.
   1978 Fatsialno-Paleoekologicheskoe Izuchenie Fossilizovannykh Ostatkov Rastenii (A Facies-Paleocological Study of Fossilized Plant Remains; in Russian). In *Voprosy Tafonomii i Paleobiologii*, Chaired by B.S. Soklov, pp. 108-115. SSSR, Akademiya Nauk, Vsesoyuznoe Paleontologicheskoe Obshchestvo. Trudy Sessi 20. Leningrad.

852. Owens, M.J., and D. Owens
   1978 Feeding Ecology and Its Influence on Social Organization in Brown Hyaenas (*Hyaena brunnea*, Thunberg) of the Central Kalahari Desert. *East African Wildlife Journal* 16:113-135.

853. Paine, G.
   1937 Fossilization of Bone. *American Journal of Science* 234:148-157.

854. Papin, Y.S., and A.A. Doroshenko
   1978 Primenenie v Taksonomii Nemorckikh Pozdnepaleozoiskikh Dvustvorok Nekotorykh Osobennostei ikh Zakhoroneniya (Certain Burial Characteristics of Upper Paleozoic Nonmarine Bivalves and Their Application in Taxonomy; in Russian). In *Voprosy Tafonomii i Paleobiologii*, Chaired by B.S. Soklov, pp. 115-119. SSSR, Akademiya Nauk, Vsesoyuznoe Paleontologicheskoe Obshchestvo. Trudy Sessi 20. Leningrad.

855. Park, E.
   1978 The Ginsberg Caper: Hacking it as in Stone Age. *Smithsonian* 9(4):85-96.

856. Parker, R.B., and H. Toots
   1970 Minor Elements in Fossil Bone. *Geological Society of America. Bulletin* 81:925-932.

857. Parker, R.B., and H. Toots
   1974 Minor Elements in Fossil Bone: Applications to Quaternary Samples. *Wyoming Geological Survey. Report of Investigations* 10:74-77.

858. Parker, R.B., and H. Toots
   1980 Trace Elements in Bones as Paleobiological Indicators. In *Fossils in the Making: Vertebrate Taphonomy and Paleoecology*, edited by A.K. Behrensmeyer and A.P. Hill, pp. 197-207. University of Chicago Press, Chicago.

859. Parrish, W.C.
   1978 Paleoenvironmental Analysis of a Lower Permian Bonebed and Adjacent Sediments, Wichita County, Texas. *Palaeogeography, Palaeoclimatology, Palaeoecology* 24:209-237.

860. Pate, D., and K.A. Brown
    1985 The Stability of Bone Strontium in the Geochemical Environment. *Journal of Human Evolution* 14:483-491.
861. Patrunov, D.K.
    1978 Premery Tekstury "Khodov" v Srednem Paleeozoe Sovetskoi Arktidi i ikh Interpretatsiya (Examples of the Texture of "Tracks" in the Middle Paleozoic of the Soviet Arctic and Their Interpretation; in Russian). In *Voprosy Tafonomii i Paleobiologii*, Chaired by B.S. Soklov, pp. 119-127. SSSR, Akademiya Nauk, Vsesoyuznoe Paleontologicheskoe Obshchestvo. Trudy Sessi 20. Leningrad.
862. Paul, C.R.C.
    1982 How Much of the Record is Fossiliferous? (Abstract). *Journal of Paleontology* 56(Supp. No. 2):20.
863. Pavlish, L.A., A.V. Jopling, and Zhang Zhenchun
    1986 Selective Transport of Stone and Bone: An Experimental Approach from Flume to Field. Manuscript on file with C.P. Koch.
864. Pavlish, L.A., and P. Sheppard
    1978 Observations on the Fracturing of Frozen Bone. Ms. on file with Northern Yukon Research Programme, Department of Anthropology, University of Toronto.
865. Pawlicki, R., A. Korbel, and H. Kubiak
    1966 Cells, Collagen Fibrils and Vessels in Dinosaur Bone. *Nature* 211:1697-1770.
866. Payne, A.G.
    1987 Comment on Blumenschine 1987, with reply. *Current Anthropology* 28:399.
867. Payne, J.A.
    1965 A Summer Carrion Study of the Baby Pig *Sus scrofa* Linnaeus. *Ecology* 46:592-602.
868. Payne, J.A., E.W. King, and G. Beinhart
    1968 Arthropod Succession and Decomposition of Buried Pigs. *Nature* 219:1180-1181.
869. Payne, J.A., F.W. Mead, and E.W. King
    1968 Hemiptera Associated with Pig Carrion. *Entomological Society of America. Annals* 61:565-567.
870. Payne, S.
    1972 On the Interpretation of Bone Samples from Archaeological Sites. In *Papers in Economic Prehistory*, edited by E. Higgs, pp. 65-81. Cambridge University Press, Cambridge.
871. Payne, S.
    1972 Partial Recovery and Sample Bias: The Results of Some Sieving Experiments In *Papers in Economic Prehistory*, edited by E. Higgs, pp. 49-64. Cambridge University Press, Cambridge.
872. Payne, S.
    1975 Partial Recovery and Sample Bias. In *Archaeozoological Studies*, edited by A.T. Clason, pp. 7-17. American Elsevier, New York.
873. Payne, S., and P.J. Munson
    1985 Ruby and How Many Squirrels? Destruction of Bones by Dogs. In *Palaeobiological Investigations: Research Design, Methods and Data Analysis*, edited by N.R.J. Fieller, D.D. Gilbertson, and N.G.A. Ralph, pp. 31-48. American Elsevier, New York.
874. Pearson, J., and J.S. Rinehart
    1952 Deformation and Fracturing of Thick-walled Steel Cylinders Under Explosive Attack. *Journal of Applied Physics* 23:434-441.
875. Pearson, O.P.
    1964 Carnivore-Mouse Predation: An Example of its Intensity and Bioenergetics. *Journal of Mammalogy* 45:177-188.
876. Pei, G.
    1985 Comment on Binford and Ho 1985 (Reply by Binford and Ho). *Current Anthropology* 26:435.
877. Pei, W.-C.
    1932 Preliminary Note on Some Incised, Cut and Broken Bones Found in Assocation with *Sinanthropus* Remains and Lithic Artifacts from Choukoutien. *Geological Society of China. Bulletin* 12:105-108.
878. Pei, W.-C.
    1938 *Le Rôle des Animaux et des Causes Naturelles dans la Cassure des Os.* Palaeontoligica Sinica, Series D, New Series No. 7 (Whole Series No. 118), Geological Survey of China, Nanking.
879. Perkins, D.
    1973 A Critique on the Methods of Quantifying Faunal Remains from Archaeological Sites. In *Domestikationsforschung und Geschichte der Haustiere*, edited by J. Matolcsi, pp. 367-370. Akademiai Kiado, Budapest.
880. Perkins, D., and P. Daly
    1968 A Hunters' Village in Neolothic Turkey. *Scientific American* 219:97-106.
881. Peterson, C.H.
    1982 Clam Predation by Whelks (*Busycon* sp.): Experimental Tests of the Importance of Prey Size, Prey Density, and Sea Grass Cover. *Marine Biology* 66:159-170.
882. Pettijohn, F.J.
    1957 *Sedimentary Rocks.* Harper Brothers, New York.
883. Péwé, T.L., and G.A. Llanos
    1959 Mummified Seal Carcasses in the MacMurdo Sound Region, Antartica. *Science* 130:176.
884. Picard, M.D., and L.R. High, Jr.
    1973 *Sedimentary Structures of Ephemeral Streams.* Developments in Sedimentology No. 17. Elsevier, Amsterdam.
885. Pidoplichko, I.G.
    1976 *Mezhirichskie Zhilishcha iz Kosti Mamonta. (Mammoth Bone Dwellings from Mezhirich).* Naukova Dumka, Kiev.
886. Piekarski, K.
    1970 Fracture of Bone. *Journal of Applied Physics* 41:215-223.

887. Piepenbrink, H.
　　1986　Two Examples of Biogenous Dead Bone Decomposition and Their Consequences for Taphonomic Interpretation. *Journal of Archaeological Science* 13:417-430.
888. Pierce, W.D.
　　1947　Fossil Arthropods of California: 14. A Progress Report on the McKittrick Asphalt Field. *Southern California Academy of Sciences. Bulletin* 46:138-143.
889. Pierce, W.D.
　　1948　Fossil Arthropods of California: 15. Some Hemiptera from the McKittrick Asphalt Field. *Southern California Academy of Sciences. Bulletin* 47:21-33.
890. Pierce, W.D.
　　1949　Fossil Arthropods of California: 17. The Silphid Burying Beetles in the Asphalt Field. *Southern California Academy of Sciences. Bulletin* 48:55-70.
891. Pimlott, D.H., J.A. Shannon, and G.B. Kolenosky
　　1969　*The Ecology of the Timber Wolf.* Ontario. Department of Lands and Forest Research Report (Wildlife) No. 87.
892. Piperno, D.R.
　　1985　Phytolith Taphonomy and Distributions in Archaeological Sediments from Panama. *Journal of Archaeological Science* 12:247-267.
893. Plug, I.
　　1978　Collecting Patterns of Six Species of Vultures (Aves: Accipitridae). *Transvaal Museum, Pretoria. Annals* 31:51-63.
894. Plug, I.
　　1984　MNI Counts, Pits and Features. In *Frontiers: Southern African Archaeology Today*, edited by M. Hall, G. Avery, D.M. Avery, M.L. Wilson, and A.J.B. Humphreys, pp. 357-362. British Archaeological Reports, BAR International Series No. 207. Oxford.
895. Poggenpoel, C.A.
　　1984　The Determination of Minimum Numbers of Individual Fish from Coastal Site s in South Africa. In *Frontiers: Southern African Archaeology Today*, edited by M. Hall, G. Avery, D.M. Avery, M.L. Wilson, and A.J.B. Humphreys, pp. 367-372. British Archaeological Reports, BAR International Series No. 207. Oxford.
896. Poplin, F.
　　1974　Deux cas particuliers de débitage par unsure. In *Colloque International sur L'Industrie de L'Os dans la Préhistorie*, 1st (Abbaye de Senanque, Gordes, France, 1974), edited by H. Camps-Fabrer, pp. 85-92. Editions de L'Université de Provence, Aix-en-Provence.
897. Poplin, F.
　　1977　Problémes d'ostéologie quantitative relatifs a l'etude de l'écologie des hommes fossiles. *Association Française Étude du Quaternaire, Supplément et Bulletin* 47:63-68.

898. Poplin, F.
　　1981　Un probleme d'ostéologie quantitative: calcul d'effectif initial d'apres appariements. Generalisation auz autres types de remontages et a d'autres matériels archéologiques. *Revue d'Archaéométrie* 5:159-165.
899. Poplin, F.
　　1983　Essai ostéologie quantitive sur l'estimation du nombre d'individus. *Kölner Jahrbuch für Vor-und Frühgeschichte* 16:153-164.
900. Potter, P.E., and F.J. Pettijohn
　　1963　*Paleocurrents and Basin Analysis.* Academic Press, New York.
901. Potts, R.B.
　　1982　*Lower Pleistocene Site Formation and Hominid Activities at Olduvai Gorge, Tanzania.* Ph.D. dissertation, Harvard University. University Microfilms 8222692, Ann Arbor.
902. Potts, R.B.
　　1983　Foraging for Faunal Resources by Early Hominids at Olduvai Gorge, Tanqiana. In *Animals and Archaeology: 1. Hunters and Their Prey*, edited by J. Clutton-Brock and C. Grigson, pp. 51-62. British Archaeological Reports, BAR International Series No. 163. Oxford.
903. Potts, R.B.
　　1984　Hominid Hunters? Problems of Identifying the Earliest Hunter/Gatherers. In *Hominid Evolution*, edited by R. Foley, pp. 129-166. Academic Press, London.
904. Potts, R.B.
　　1986　Temporal Span of Bone Accumulations at Olduvai Gorge and Implications for Early Hominid Foraging Behavior. *Paleobiology* 12:25-31.
905. Potts, R.B.
　　1987　On Butchery by Olduvai Hominids (Comment on Bunn and Kroll 1986, reply by Bunn and Kroll). *Current Anthropology* 28:95-98.
906. Potts, R.B., and P.L. Shipman
　　1981　Cutmarks Made by Stone Tools on Bones from Olduvai Gorge, Tanzania. *Nature* 291:577-580.
907. Potts, R.B., P.L. Shipman, and E. Ingall
　　1985　Taphonomy, Paleoecology, and Hominids of Lainyamok, Kenya. Paper presented to the American Association of Physical Anthropologists, Knoxville, Tennessee.
908. Pozorski, S.
　　1979　Late Prehistoric Llama Remains from the Moche Valley, Peru. *Carnegie Museum, Pittsburgh. Annals* 48:139-170.
909. Price, T.D.
　　1985　Late Archaic Subsistence in the Midwestern United States. *Journal of Human Evolution* 14:449-459.
910. Price, T.D., M.J. Schoeninger, and G.J. Armelagos
　　1985　Bone Chemistry and Past Behavior: An Overview. *Journal of Human Evolution* 14:419-447.
911. Putnam, F.W.
　　1906　Evidence of the Work of Man on Objects from Quaternary Caves in California. *American Anthropologist* 8:229-235.

912. Raczynski, J., and A.L. Ruprecht
    1974 The Effect of Digestion on the Osteological Composition of Owl Pellets. *Acta Ornithologica* 14:25-38.
913. Ragan, D.M.
    1968 *Structural Geology: An Introduction to Geometrical Techniques*. John Wiley, New York.
914. Rancier, J., G.A. Haynes, and D. Stanford
    1982 1981 Investigations of Lamb Spring. *Southwestern Lore* 48:1-17.
915. Rapson, D.J.
    1984 Reivew of *Bison Kills and Bone Counts: Decision Making by Ancient Hunters*, by J.D. Speth. *Journal of Anthropological Research* 40:339-341.
916. Raup, D.M., and R.E. Crick
    1979 Measurement of Faunal Similarity in Paleontology. *Journal of Paleontology* 53:1213-1227.
917. Raup, D.M., and S.M. Stanley
    1971 *Principles of Paleontology*. W.H. Freeman, San Franciso.
918. Read, C.E.
    1971 *Animal Bones and Human Behavior: Approaches to Faunal Analysis in Archeology*. Ph.D. dissertation, University of California, Los Angeles. University Microfilms 71-21,336, Ann Arbor.
919. Read-Martin, C.E.
    1974 *Animal Remains and Hunting Behavior: Faunal Analysis for Some American Assemblages*. University of California, Los Angeles. Archaeological Survey Report No. 14.
920. Read-Martin, C.E., and D.W. Read
    1975 Australopithecine Scavenging and Human Evolution: An Approach from Faunal Analysis. *Current Anthropology* 16:359-365.
921. Read-Martin, C.E., and D.W. Read
    1975 Reply to Bonnichsen. *Current Anthropology* 16:635-636.
922. Read-Martin, C.E., and D.W. Read
    1976 More on Faunal Analysis. (Reply to Shipman and Phillips 1976). *Current Anthropology* 17:531-533.
923. Redding, R.W., J.W. Pires-Ferreira, and M.A. Zeder
    1976/77 A Proposed System for Computer Analysis of Identifiable Faunal Material from Archaeological Sites. *Paleorient* 3:191-205.
924. Redding, R.W., M.A. Zeder, and J.E. McArdle
    1978 "Bonesort II" — A System for the Computer Processing of Indentifiable Faunal Material. *Peabody Museum of Archaeology and Ethnology. Bulletins* 2:135-147.
925. Reed, C.A.
    1963 Osteo-Archaeology. In *Science in Archaeology*, edited by D. Brothwell and E. Higgs, pp. 204-216. Thames and Hudson, London.
926. Reed, C.I., and B.P. Reed
    1928 The Mechanism of Pellet Formation in the Great Horned Owl *(Bubo virginianus)*. *Science* 68:359-360. 68:359-360.
927. Reed, H.B.
    1958 A Study of Dog Carcass Communities in Tennessee, with Special Reference to the Insects. *American Midland Naturalist* 59:213-245.
928. Reher, C.A.
    1970 Population Dynamics of the Glenrock *Bison bison* Population. In *The Glenrock Buffalo Jump 48C0304*, by G.C. Frison, pp. 51-55. Plains Anthropologist Memoir No. 7, Appendix II.
929. Reif, W.-E.
    1971 Zur Genese des Muschelkalk-Keuper-Grenzbonebeds in Südwestdeutschland (English summary). *Neues Jarbuch für Geologie und Paläontologie. Abhandlungen* 139:369-404.
930. Reif, W.-E.
    1978 Plicae and Cardinal-crurae in Pectinids: Protective Devices Against Starfish Predation? *Neues Jahrbuch für Geologie und Paläontologie. Abhandlungen* 157:115-118.
931. Reineck, H.E., and I.B. Singh
    1973 *Depositional Sedimentary Environments*. Springer-Verlag, New York.
932. Retallack, G.J.
    1984 Trace Fossils of Burrowing Beetles and Bees in an Oligocene Paleosol, Badlands National Park, South Dakota. *Journal of Paleontology* 58:571-592.
933. Reynolds, T.E.G.
    1986 On the Agents of Bone Accumulation at Zhoukoudian. (Comment on Binford and Ho 1985, Reply by Binford). *Current Anthropology* 27:368-369.
934. Richardson, P.R.K.
    1980 Carnivore Damage to Antelope Bones and its Archaeological Implications. *Palaeontologia Africana* 23:109-125.
935. Rick, J.W.
    1976 Downslope Movement and Archaeological Intrasite Analysis. *American Antiquity* 41:133-144.
936. Richter, R.
    1928 Aktuopaläontologie und Paläobiologie. *Senkenbergiana* 10:285-292.
937. Rigby, J.K.
    1958 Frequency Curves and Death Relationships Among Fossils. *Journal of Paleontology* 32:1007-1009.
938. Robinson, J.T.
    1959 A Bone Implement from Sterkfontein. *Nature* 184:583-585.
939. Robinson, J.T.
    1962 Australopithecines and Artifacts at Sterkfontein. *South African Archaeological Bulletin* 17:87-107.
940. Rodriguez, J., and Gutschick
    1977 Barnacle Borings in Live and Dead Hosts from the Louisiana Limestone (Famennian) of Missouri. *Journal of Paleontology* 51:718-724.
941. Rodriguez, W.C., and W.M. Bass
    1983 Insect Activity and its Relationship to Decay Rates of Human Cadavers in East Tennessee. *Journal of Forensic Sciences* 28:423-432.

942. Rodriguez, W.C., and W.M. Bass
    1985 Decomposition of Buried Bodies and Methods That May Aid in Their Location. *Journal of Forensic Sciences* 30:836-852.
943. Roe, F.G.
    1951 *The North American Buffalo*. University of Toronto Press, Toronto.
944. Roger, J.
    1974 *Paléontologie Générale*. Masson, Paris.
945. Rogers, A.F.
    1924 Mineralogy and Petrography of Fossil Bone. *Geological Society of America. Bulletin* 35:535-556.
946. Rogers, E.S.
    1973 *The Quest for Food and Furs by the Mistassini Cree, 1953-1954*. National Museum of Man, Ottawa. Publications in Ethnology No. 5.
947. Rolfe, W.D.I., and D.W. Brett
    1969 Fossilization Processes. In *Organic Geochemistry Methods and Results*, edited by G. Eglinton and M.T.J. Murphy, pp. 213-244. Springer-Verlag, Berlin.
948. Rollins, H.B., and J. Donohue
    1975 Towards a Theoretical Basis of Paleoecology: Concepts of Community Dynamics. *Lethaia* 8:256-269.
949. Romer, A.S., N.E. Wright, T. Edinger, and R. Van Frank
    1962 *Bibliography of Fossil Vertebrates Exclusive of North America. 1590-1927*. Vols. 1 and 2. Geological Society of America. Memoirs 87.
950. Roper, D.C.
    1976 Lateral Displacement of Artifacts Due to Plowing. *American Antiquity* 41:372-375.
951. Roper, M.K.
    1969 A Survey of the Evidence for Intrahuman Killing in the Pleistocene. *Current Anthropology* 10:427-459.
952. Rose, J.J.
    1983 A Replication Technique for Scanning Electron Microscopy: Applications for Anthropologists. *American Journal of Physical Anthropology* 62:255-261.
953. Rouse, I., and J.M. Cruxent
    1963 *Venezuelan Archaeology*. Yale University Press, New Haven.
954. Ruangwit, U.
    1967 The Split-Line Phenomenon and the Microscopic Structure of Bone. *American Journal of Physical Anthropology* 26:325-334.
955. Rudberg, S.
    1961/62 A Report on Some Field Observations Concerning Periglacial Geomorphology and Mass Movement on Slopes in Sweden. *Biuletyn Peryglacjalny* 10/11:311-323.
956. Runnings, A.L., C.E. Gustafson, and D. Bently
    1989 Use-Wear on Bone Tools: A Technique for the Study Under the Scanning Electron Microscope. In *Bone Modification*, edited by R. Bonnichsen and M. Sorg (1st International Bone Modification Conference, Proceedings). Center for the Study of the First Americans, Orono, Maine.
957. Russell, M.D.
    1987 Bone Breakage in the Krapina Hominid Collection. *American Journal of Physical Anthropology* 72:381-397.
958. Russell, M.D.
    1987 Mortuary Practices at the Krapina Neandertal Site. *American Journal of Physical Anthropology* 72:373-379.
959. Russell, M.D., and F. LeMort
    1986 Cutmarks on the Engis 2 Calvaria? *American Journal of Physical Anthropology* 69:317-323.
960. Sadek-Kooros, H.
    1966 *Jaguar Cave: An Early Man Site in the Beaverhead Mountains of Idaho*. Ph.D. dissertation, Harvard University.
961. Sadek-Kooros, H.
    1972 Primitive Bone Fracturing: A Method of Research. *American Antiquity* 37:369-382.
962. Sadek-Kooros, H.
    1975 Intentional Fracturing of Bone: Description of Criteria. In *Archaeozoological Studies*, edited by A.T. Clason, pp. 139-150. American Elsevier, New York.
963. Sagan, E.
    1974 *Cannibalism: Human Aggression and Cultural Form*. Harper and Row, New York.
964. Saunders, J.J.
    1977 *Late Pleistocene Vertebrates of the Western Ozark Highland*. Reports of Investigations No. 33. Illinois State Museum.
965. Saunders, J.K.
    1963 Food Habits of the Lynx in Newfoundland. *Journal of Wildlife Management* 27:384-390.
966. Savage, H.
    1972 Faunal Findings at the Constance Bay Site No. 1 (BiGa-2). *Ontario Archaeological Society. Publications* 18:25-36.
967. Schäfer, W.
    1955 Fossilisations — Bedingungen der Meeressäuger und Vögel. *Senckenbergiana Lethaea* 36:1-25.
968. Schäfer, W.
    1977 *Ecology and Palaeoecology of Marine Environments*. Oliver and Boyd, Edinburgh.
969. Scherer, M., and J. Wendt
    1978 Diagenese Oberpermischer Kalkschwämme aus Patch-Reefs des Djebel Tebaga (S-Tunesien). *Neues Jahrbuch für Geologie und Paläontologie. Abhandlungen* 157:196-202.
970. Schick, K.D.
    1984 *Processes of Palaeolithic Site Formation: An Experimental Study*. Ph.D. dissertation, University of California, Berkeley. University Microfilms DA8427088, Ann Arbor.
971. Schick, K.D.
    1986 *Stone Age Sites in the Making Experiments in the Formation and Transformation of Archaeological Occurrences*. British Archaeological Reports, BAR International Series No. 319, Oxford.

972. Schick, K.D., N. Toth, and M.E. Daeschler
1989 An Early Paleontological Assemblage as an Archaeological Test Case. In *Bone Modification*, edited by R. Bonnichsen and M. Sorg (1st International Bone Modification Conference, Proceedings). Center for the Study of the First Americans, Orono, Maine.

973. Schoeninger, M.J.
1985 Trophic Level Effects on 15N/14N and 13C/12C Ratios in Bone Collagen and Strontium Levels in Bone Mineral. *Journal of Human Evolution* 14:515-525.

974. Schopf, J.M.
1975 Models of Fossil Preservation. *Review of Palaeobotany and Palynology* 20:27-53.

975. Schumm, S.A., and M.A. Stevens
1973 Abrasion in Place: A Mechanism for Rounding and Size Reduction of Coarse Sediments in Rivers. *Geology* 1:37-40.

976. Schwartz, H.L.
1983 *Paleoecology of Late Cenozoic Fishes from the Turkana Basin, Northern Kenya*. Ph.D. dissertation, University of California, Santa Cruz. University Microfilms DA8406993, Ann Arbor.

977. Scott, K.
1980 Two Hunting Episodes of Middle Palaeolithic Age at La Cotte de Saint-Brelade, Jersey (Channel Islands). *World Archaeology* 12:137-152.

978. Scott, K.
1989 Mammoth Bones Modified by Man: Evidence from La Cotte de St. Brelade, Jersey, Channel Islands. In *Bone Modification*, edited by R. Bonnichsen and M. Sorg (1st International Bone Modification Conference, Proceedings). Center for the Study of the First Americans, Orono, Maine.

979. Scott, L., and R.G. Klein
1981 A Hyena-accumulated Bone Assemblage from Late Holocene Deposits at Deelpan, Orange Free State. *South African Museum. Annals* 86:217-227.

980. Scott, R.W., and R.R. West
1976 *Structure and Classification of Paleocommunities*. Dowden, Hutchinson and Ross, Stroudsburg, Pennsylvania.

981. Scotter, G.W., and N.M. Simmons
1976 Mortality of Dall's Sheep Within a Cave. *Journal of Mammalogy* 57:387-389.

982. Scrivner, P.J., and D.J. Bottjer
1986 Neogene Avian and Mammalian Tracks from Death Valley National Monument, California: Their Context, Classification and Preservation. *Palaeogeography, Paleoclimatology, Palaeoecology* 57:285-331.

983. Seidensticker, J.
1983 Predation by *Panthera* Cats and Measures of Human Influence in Habitats of South Asian Monkeys. *International Journal of Primatology* 4:323-326.

984. Seilacher, A.
1964 Biogenic Sedimentary Structures. In *Approaches to Paleoecology*, edited by J. Imbrie and N. Newell, pp. 296-316. John Wiley, New York.

985. Seilacher, A.
1973 Biostratinomy: The Sedimentology of Biologically Standardized Particles. In *Evolving Concepts in Sedimentology*, edited by R.N. Ginsburg, pp. 159-177. Johns Hopkins University Studies in Geology No. 21. Baltimore.

986. Seilacher, A.
1978 Evolution of Trace Fossil Communities in the Deep Sea. *Neues Jahrbuch für Geologie und Paläontologie. Abhandlungen* 157:251-255.

987. Seilacher, A., and K. Brenner
1978 New Aspects about the Origin of the Toarcian Posidonia Shales. *Neues Jahrbuch Für Geologie und Paläontologie. Abhandlungen* 157:11-18. 157:11-18.

988. Seilacher, A., and E. Wiesenauer
1978 Preservational and Depositional History of Belemnites. *Neues Jahrbuch für Geologie und Paläontologie. Abhandlungen* 157:145-149.

989. Seilacher, A.
1983 Upper Paleozoic Trace Fossils from the Gilf Kebir-Aburas Area in Southwestern Egypt. *Journal of African Earth Sciences* 1:21-34.

990. Sekulic, R., and R.D. Estes
1977 A Note on Bone Chewing in the Sable Antelope in Kenya. *Mammalia* 41:537-539.

991. Semenov, S.A.
1964 *Prehistoric Technology*. Translated by M.W. Thompson. Barnes and Noble, New York.

992. Sepkoski, J.J.
1979 Taphonomic Factors Influencing the Lithologic Occurrence of Fossils in Dresbachian (Upper Cambrian) Shaley Facies. *Geological Society of America. Abstracts* 10:490.

993. Shackleford, J.M., and R.W.G. Wyckoff
1964 Collagen in Fossil Teeth and Bones. *Journal of Ultrastructure Research* 11:173-180.

994. Shackley, M.L.
1974 Stream Abrasion of Flint. *Nature* 248:501-502.

995. Shackley, M.L.
1975 *Archaeological Sediments: A Survey of Analytical Methods*. Butterworths, London.

996. Shackley, M.L.
1978 The Behaviour of Artefacts as Sedimentary Particles in a Fluviatile Environment. *Archaeometry* 20:55-61.

997. Shalimov, A.I.
1978 Sledy Zheznedeyatelnosti Organiemov v Terrigennom Flishe Tavricheskoi Sepii (Gornyi Krym) i ikh Paleogeograficheskoe Znachenie (Tracks of Living Organisms in Terrigeneous Flysch of the Tavricheskaya Suite (Crimean Mountains) and Their Paleogeographical Importance; in Russian). In *Voprosy Tafonomii i Paleobiologii*, Chaired by B.S. Soklov, pp. 142-149. SSSR, Akademiya Nauk, Veseoyuznoe Paleontologicheskoe Obshchestvo. Trudy Sessi 20. Leningrad.

998. Shchegolev, A.K.
1978 Znachenie Tafonomicheskikh Issledovanii Rastitelnykh Ostatkov dlya Opredeleniya Skorosti Osadkonakopleniya (Taphonomic Studies of Plant Remains for Determining the Velocity of Deposition; in Russian). In *Voprosy Tafonomii i Paleobiologii*, Chaired by B.S. Soklov, pp. 149-153. SSSR, Akademiya Nauk, Veseoyuznoe Paleontologicheskoe Obshchestvo. Trudy Sessi 20. Leningrad.

999. Shipman, P.L.
1975 Implications of Drought from Vertebrate Fossil Assemblages. *Nature* 257:667-668.

1000. Shipman, P.L.
1977 *Paleoecology, Taphonomic History, and Population Dynamics of the Vertebrate Fossil Assemblage from the Middle Miocene Deposits Exposed at Fort Ternan, Kenya*. Ph.D. dissertation, New York University. University Microfilms 780314, Ann Arbor.

1001. Shipman, P.L.
1977 A Reconstruction of the Taphonomic History and Paleoecology of the Fort Ternan Assemblage. Paper presented at the 46th annual meeting of the American Association of Physical Anthropologists, Seattle.

1002. Shipman, P.L.
1978 Patterns of Bone Breakage and Early Human Behavior. Paper presented at the 47th annual meeting of the American Association of Physical Anthropologists, Toronto.

1003. Shipman, P.L.
1979 Microscopic Effects of Known Taphonomic Events on Bones and Teeth. Paper presented at the 48th annual meeting of the American Association of Physical Anthropologists, San Francisco.

1004. Shipman, P.L.
1981 *Life History of a Fossil: An Introduction to Taphonomy and Paleoecology*. Harvard University Press, Cambridge.

1005. Shipman, P.L.
1981 Applications of Scanning Electron Microscopy to Taphonomic Problems. *New York Academy of Sciences. Annals* 376:357-386.

1006. Shipman, P.L.
1982 Reconstructing the Paleoecology and Taphonomic History of Ramapithecus wickeri at Fort Ternan, Kenya. University of Missouri, Columbia. Museum of Anthropology. Museum Brief No. 26.

1007. Shipman, P.L.
1983 Early Hominid Lifestyle: Hunting and Gathering or Foraging and Scavenging? In *Animals and Archaeology: 1. Hunters and Their Prey*, edited by J. Clutton-Brock and C. Grigson, pp. 31-49. British Archaeological Reports, BAR International Series No. 163. Oxford.

1008. Shipman, P.L.
1985 The Ancestor that Wasn't. *The Sciences* 25:42-48.

1009. Shipman, P.L.
1986 Scavenging or Hunting in Early Hominids: Theoretical Framework and Tests. *American Anthropologist* 88:27-42.

1010. Shipman, P.L.
1986 Studies of Hominid-Faunal Interactions at Olduvai Gorge. *Journal of Human Evolution* 15:691-706.

1011. Shipman, P.L.
1989 Altered Bones from Olduvai Gorge, Tanzania: Technical Problems, and Implications of Their Recognition. In *Bone Modification*, edited by R. Bonnichsen and M. Sorg (1st International Bone Modification Conference, Proceedings). Center for the Study of the First Americans, Orono, Maine.

1012. Shipman, P.L., W. Bosler, and K.L. Davis
1981 Butchering of Giant Geladas at an Acheulian Site. *Current Anthropology* 22:257-268.

1013. Shipman, P.L., W. Bosler, and K.L. Davis
1982 (Reply to Binford and Todd 1982). *Current Anthropology* 23:110-111.

1014. Shipman, P.L., K.L. Davis, and W. Bosler
cf 1982 The Striped Hyena *(Hyaena hyaena)* as a Collector of Bones. Ms. on file with C.P. Koch.

1015. Shipman, P.L., D.C. Fisher, and J.J. Rose
1984 Mastodon Butchery: Microscopic Evidence of Carcass Processing and Bone Tool Use. *Paleobiology* 10:358-365.

1016. Shipman, P.L., G. Foster, and M. Schoeninger
1984 Burnt Bones and Teeth: An Experimental Study of Color, Morphology, Crystal Structure and Shrinkage. *Journal of Archaeological Science* 11:307-325.

1017. Shipman, P.L., and J.E. Phillips
1975 Similarities Between a Modern Bone Assemblage and Osteodontokeratic Tools from Makapan. Paper presented at the 44th annual meeting of the American Association of Physical Anthropologists, Denver.

1018. Shipman, P.L., and J.E. Phillips
1976 On Scavenging by Hominids and Other Carnivores. *Current Anthropology* 17:170-172.

1019. Shipman, P.L., and J.E. Phillips-Conroy
1977 Hominid Tool-Making Versus Carnivore Scavenging. *American Journal of Physical Anthropology* 46:77-86.

1020. Shipman, P.L., and J.J. Rose.
1983 Early Hominid Hunting, Butchering, and Carcass-Processing Behaviors: Approaches to the Fossil Record. *Journal of Anthropological Archaeology* 2:57-98.

1021. Shipman, P.L., and J.J. Rose
1984 Cutmark Mimics on Modern and Fossil Bovid Bones. *Current Anthropology* 25:116-117.

1022. Shipman, P.L., and A.C. Walker
1980 Bone-Collecting by Harvesting Ants. *Paleobiology* 6:496-502.

1023. Shipman, P.L., A.C. Walker, J.A. Van Couvering, P.J. Hooker, and J.A. Miller
1981 The Fort Ternan Hominoid Site, Kenya: Geology, Age, Taphonomy and Paleoecology. *Journal of Human Evolution* 10:49-72.

1024. Shotwell, J.A.
1955 An Approach to the Paleoecology of Mammals. *Ecology* 39:327-337.

1025. Shotwell, J.A.
    1958 Inter-Community Relationships in Hemphillian (Mid-Pliocene) Mammals. *Ecology* 39:271-282.
1026. Shrock, R.R.
    1948 *Sequence in Layered Rock*. McGraw-Hill, New York.
1027. Siegfried, W.R.
    1984 An Analysis of Faecal Pellets of the Brown Hyaena on the Namib Coast. *South African Journal of Zoology* 19:61.
1028. Sillero-Zubiri, C., and M.D. Gottelli
    1987 *The Ecology of Spotted Hyaena in The Salient, Aberdare N.P., and Recommendations for Wildlife Management*. Report for Wildlife Conservation and Management Department, Ministry of Tourism and Wildlife, Kenya.
1029. Simons, D.B., and E.V. Richardson
    1961 Forms of Bed Roughness in Alluvial Channels. *American Society of Civil Engineers. Hydraulics Division. Journal* 87:87-105.
1030. Simons, D.B., and E.V. Richardson
    1966 *Resistance to Flow in Alluvial Channels*. U.S. Geological Survey. Professional Paper No. 422-J.
1031. Simons, D.B., E.V. Richardson, and M.L. Albertson
    1961 *Flume Studies Using Medium Sand*. U.S. Geological Survey. Water Supply Paper No. 1498-A.
1032. Simons, D.B., E.V. Richardson, and C.F. Nordin
    1965 Sedimentary Structures Generated by Flow in Alluvial Channels. In *Primary Sedimentary Structures and Their Hydrodynamic Interpretation*, edited by G.V. Middleton, pp. 34-52. Special Publications No. 12. Society of Economic Paleontologists and Mineralogists.
1033. Simons, J.W.
    1966 The Presence of Leopard and a Study of the Food Debris in the Leopard Lairs of the Mount Suswa Caves, Kenya. *Cave Exploration Group of East Africa. Bulletin* 1:51-69.
1034. Simpson, G.G.
    1926 Mesozoic Mammalia: 4. The Multituberculates as Living Animals. *American Journal of Science* 11:228-250.
1035. Sinclair, W.J., and W. Granger
    1914 Paleocene Deposits of the San Juan Basin, New Mexico. *American Museum of Natural History. Bulletin* 33:297-316.
1036. Singer, R.
    1956 The "Bone Tools" from Hopefield. *American Anthropologist* 58:1127-1134.
1037. Sisson, S., and J.D. Grossman
    1953 *The Anatomy of the Domestic Animals*. W.B. Saunders, Philadelphia.
1038. Skerlj, B.
    1939 Kannibalismus in Altpaläolithikum? *Quartär* 2:108-119.
1039. Skinner, J.D.
    1976 Ecology of the Brown Hyena *Hyena brunnea* in the Transvaal with a Distribution Map for Southern Africa. *South African Journal of Science* 72:262-269.
1040. Skinner, J.D., S. Davis, and G. Ilani
    1980 Bone Collecting by Striped Hyaenas, *Hyaena hyaena*, in Israel. *Palaeontologia Africana* 23:99-104.
1041. Skinner, J.D., and G. Ilani
    1979 The Striped Hyaena *(Hyaena hyaena)* of the Judean and Negev Deserts and a Comparison with the Brown Hyaena *(Hyaena brunnea)*. *Israel Journal of Zoology* 28:229-232.
1042. Skinner, J.D., and R.J. Van Aarde
    1981 The Distribution and Ecology of the Brown Hyaena *(Hyaena brunnea)* and Spotted Hyaena *(Hyaena crocuta)* in the Central Namib Desert. *Madoqua* 12:231-239.
1043. Smith, B.D.
    1975 Toward a More Accurate Estimation of the Meat Yield of Animal Species at Archaeological Sites. In *Archaeozoological Studies*, edited by A.T. Clason, pp. 99-106. American Elsevier, New York.
1044. Smith, J.W., and R. Walmsley
    1959 Factors Affecting the Elasticity of Bone. *Journal of Anatomy* 93:503-523.
1045. Smith, R.M.H.
    1980 The Lithology, Sedimentology and Taphonomy of Flood-Plain Deposits of the Lower Beaufort (Adelaide Subgroup) Strata near Beaufort West. *Geological Society of South Africa. Transactions* 83:399-413.
1046. Smith R.M.H.
    1987 Helical Burrow Casts of Therapsid Origin from the Beaufort Group (Permian) of South Africa. *Paleogeography, Paleoclimatology, Paleoecology* 60:155-170.
1047. Solomon, S., M. Minnegal, and D.P. Dwyer
    1986 Bower Birds, Bones and Archaeology. *Journal of Archaeological Science* 13:307-318.
1048. Solorzano, F.
    1989 Fossil Artifacts from State of Jalisco, Mexico, and Their Comparison with Some Prehispanic Artifacts. In *Bone Modification*, edited by R. Bonnichsen and M. Sorg (1st International Bone Modification Conference, Proceedings). Center for the Study of the First Americans, Orono, Maine.
1049. Spencer, B., and R.H. Walcott
    1911 The Origin of Cuts on Bones of Australian Extinct Marsupials. *Royal Society of Victoria. Proceedings* New Series, 24(1):92-123.
1050. Speth, J.D.
    1983 *Bison Kills and Bone Counts*. University of Chicago Press, Chicago.
1051. Spinage, C.A.
    1972 African Ungulate Life Tables. *Ecology* 53:645-652.
1052. Stallibras, S.
    1984 The Distinction Between the Effects of Small Carnivores and Humans on Post-glacial Faunal Assemblages. In *Animals and Archaeology: 4. Husbandry in Europe*, edited by C. Grigson and J. Clutton-Brock, pp. 259-269. British Archaeological Reports, BAR International Series No. 227. Oxford.

1053. Stanford, D., R. Bonnichsen, and R.E. Morlan
    1981 The Ginsburg Experiment: Modern and Prehistoric Evidence of a Bone-Flaking Technology. *Science* 212:438-440.
1054. Steele, D.G., and D.L. Carlson
    1989 Excavation and Taphonomy of Mammoth Remains from the Duewal Newberry Site, Brazos County, Texas. In *Bone Modification*, edited by R. Bonnichsen and M. Sorg (1st International Bone Modification Conference, Proceedings). Center for the Study of the First Americans, Orono, Maine.
1055. Stein, J.K.
    1983 Earthworm Activity: A Source of Potential Disturbance of Archaeological Sediments. *American Antiquity* 48:277-289.
1056. Stockton, E.D.
    1973 Shaw's Creek Shelter: Human Displacement of Artifacts and its Significance. *Mankind* 9:112-117.
1057. Stoddart, L.C.
    1970 A Telemetric Method for Detecting Jackrabbit Mortality. *Journal of Wildlife Management* 34:501-507.
1058. Stokes, W.L.
    1978 Transported Fossil Biota of the Green River Formation, Utah. *Palaeogeography, Palaeoclimatology, Palaeoecology* 25:353-364.
1059. Stout, S.D.
    1978 Histological Structure and its Preservation in Ancient Bone. *Current Anthropology* 19:601-604.
1060. Strahler, A.N.
    1952 Dynamic Basis of Geomorphology. *Geological Society of America. Bulletin* 63:923-938.
1061. Straus, L.G.
    1982 Carnivores and Cave Sites in Cantabrian Spain. *Journal of Anthropological Research* 38:45-96.
1062. Straus, L.G.
    1985 Comment on Binford and Ho 1985 (Reply by Binford and Ho). *Current Anthropology* 26:435.
1063. Sutcliffe, A.J.
    1970 A Section of an Imaginary Bone Cave. *Studies in Speleology* 2:79-80.
1064. Sutcliffe, A.J.
    1970 Spotted Hyena: Crusher, Gnawer, Digestor and Collector of Bones. *Nature* 227:1110-1113.
1065. Sutcliffe, A.J.
    1973 Similarity of Bones and Antlers Gnawed by Deer to Human Artefacts. *Nature* 246:428-430.
1066. Sutcliffe, A.J.
    1973 Caves of the East African Rift Valley. *Cave Research Group of Great Britain. Transactions* 15:41-65.
1067. Sutcliffe, A.J.
    1977 Further Notes on Bones and Antlers Chewed by Deer and Other Ungulates. *Deer* 4:73-82.
1068. Sutcliffe, A.J., and H.D. Collings
    1972 Gnawed Bones from the Crag and Forest Bed Deposits of East Anglia. *Suffolk Natural History* 15:497-498.

1069. Tanabe, K., A. Inazumi, K. Tamahama, and T. Katsuta
    1984 Taphonomy of Half Compressed Ammonites from the Lower Jurassic Black Shales of the Toyora Area, West Japan. *Palaeogeography, Palaeoclimatology, Palaeoecology* 47:329-346.
1070. Tappen, N.C.
    1953 A Functional Analysis of the Facial Skeleton with Split-Line Technique. *American Journal of Physical Anthropology* 11:503-532.
1071. Tappen, N.C.
    1964 An Examination of Alternative Explanations of Split-Line Orientation in Compact Bone. *American Journal of Physical Anthropology* 22:423-442.
1072. Tappen, N.C.
    1969 The Relationship of Weathering Cracks to Split-Line Orientation in Bone. *American Journal of Physical Anthropology* 31:191-198.
1073. Tappen, N.C.
    1970 Structure of Bone in the Skulls of Neanderthal Fossils. *American Journal of Physical Anthropology* 38:93-98.
1074. Tappen, N.C.
    1971 Two Orientational Features of Compact Bone as Predictors of Split-Line Patterns. *American Journal of Physical Anthropology* 35:129-140.
1075. Tappen, N.C.
    1979 Studies on the Condition and Structure of Bone of the Saldanha Fossil Cranium. *American Journal of Physical Anthropology* 50:591-604.
1076. Tappen, N.C.
    1987 Circum-mortem Damage to Some Ancient African Hominid Craina: A Taphonomic and Evolutionary Essay. *African Archaeological Review* 5:39-47.
1077. Tappen, N.C., and G.R. Peske
    1970 Weathering Cracks and Split-line Patterns in Archaeological Bone. *American Antiquity* 35:383-386.
1078. Tasch, P.
    1965 Communications Theory and the Fossil Record of Invertebrates. *Kansas Academy of Science. Transactions* 68:322-329.
1079. Tasch, P.
    1973 *Paleobiology of the Invertebrates*. John Wiley, New York.
1080. Taylor, J.H.
    1964 Some Aspects of Diagenesis. *Advancement of Science* 20:417-436.
1081. Teichert, C., and D.L. Serventy
    1947 Deposits of Shells Transported by Birds. *American Journal of Science* 245:322-328.
1082. Thackeray, J.F.
    1984 A Conceptual Framework in Faunal Analysis. In *Frontiers: Southern African Archaeology Today*, edited by M. Hall, G. Avery, D.M. Avery, M.L. Wilson, and A.J.B. Humphreys, pp. 349-351. British Archaeological Reports, BAR International Series No. 207. Oxford.
1083. Thomas, D.H.
    1971 On Distinguishing Natural from Cultural Bone in Archaeological Sites. *American Antiquity* 36:366-371.

1084. Thomas, G.
1950 Processes of Fossilization. *New Biology* 8:75-97.

1085. Thompson, D.Q.
1952 Travel, Range and Food Habits of Timber Wolves in Wisconsin. *Journal of Mammalogy* 33:429-442.

1086. Thorson, R.M., and R.D. Guthrie
1984 River Ice as a Taphonomic Agent: An Alternative Hypothesis for Bone "Artifacts." *Quaternary Research* 22:172-188.

1087. Thurman, M.D., and L.J. Willmore
1980/81 A Replicative Cremation Experiment. *North American Archaeologist* 2:275-283.

1088. Tilson, R.L., and J.R. Henschel
1986 Spatial Arrangement of Spotted Hyaena Groups in a Desert Environment, Namibia. *African Journal of Ecology* 24:471.

1089. Tobias, P.V.
1965 *Australopithecus, Homo habilis*, Tool-Using and Tool-Making. *South African Archaeological Bulletin* 20:167-192.

1090. Tobias, P.V.
1971 The Cultural Capacity of *Australopithecus*. In *The Brain in Hominid Evolution*, pp. 124-133. Columbia University Press, New York.

1091. Tobias, P.V.
1983 The Scientific Contributions of Raymond Dart. *Physical Anthropology News* 2(2):1-4.

1092. Todd, L.C.
1983 Taphonomy: Fleshing Out the Dry Bones of Plains Prehistory. *Wyoming Archaeologist* 26:36-46.

1093. Todd, L.C.
1986 Comment on Binford and Stone 1986. *Current Anthropology* 27:471.

1094. Manuscript deleted from bibliography.

1095. Tomenchuk, J., and S. Tomenchuk
1976 Quantifying Continuous Lesions and Fractures on Long Bones: The Design and Operation of an Inking Collar. *Journal of Field Archaeology* 3:353-355.

1096. Tooby, J.
1987 Comment on Blumenschine 1987, with reply. *Current Anthropology* 28:399-400.

1097. Toots, H.
1963 The Chemistry of Fossil Bones from Wyoming and Adjacent States. *Contributions to Geology* 2:69-80.

1098. Toots, H.
1965 Orientation and Distribution of Fossils as Environmental Indicators. *Guidebook, 19th Field Conference: Sedimentation of Lake Cretaceous and Tertiary Outcrops, Rock Springs Uplift*, pp. 219-229. Wyoming Geological Survey.

1099. Toots, H.
1965 Sequence of Disarticulations in Mammalian Skeletons. *Contributions to Geology* 4:37-39.

1100. Toots, H.
1965 Random Orientation of Fossils and its Significance. *Contributions to Geology* 4:59-62.

1101. Toy, T.J.
1977 Hillslope Form and Climate. *Geological Society of America. Bulletin* 88:16-22.

1102. Trewin, N.H., and W. Welsh
1972 Transport, Breakage and Sorting of the Bivalve *Mactra corallina* on Aberdeen Beach, Scotland. *Palaeogeography, Palaeoclimatology, Palaeoecology* 12:193-204.

1103. Trinkaus, E.
1985 Cannibalism and Burial at Krapina. *Journal of Human Evolution* 14:203-216.

1104. Trusheim, F.
1931 Versuche uber Transport und Ablagerung von Mollusken. *Senckenbergiana* 13:124-139.

1105. Tsekhovskiy, Yu.G.
1978 Sledy Zhznudeyatelnosti Zhivotnykh i Rastelnykh Organiemov v Iskopaemykh Pochvakh Pozdnemelovoi-Paleotsenovoi Savanny Kazakhstana (Tracks of Animal and Plant Life Found in Fossils of Upper Cretaceous-Paleocene Savannahs of Kazakhstan; in Russian). In *Voprosy Tafonomii i Paleobiologii*, Chaired by B.S. Soklov, pp. 136-142. SSSR, Akademiya Nauk, Vsesoyuznoe Paleontologicheskoe Obshchestvo. Trudy Sessi 20. Leningrad.

1106. Turner, A.
1980 Minimum Number Estimation Offers Minimal Insight in Faunal Analysis. *Ossa* 7:199-201.

1107. Turner, A.
1981 Predation and Palaeolithic Man in Northern England. In *Prehistoric Communities in Northern England*, edited by G.W.W. Barker, pp. 11-26. University of Sheffield, Department of Prehistory and Archaeology.

1108. Turner, A.
1983 The Quantification of Relative Abundance in Fossil and Sub-Fossil Assemblages. *Transvaal Museum, Pretoria. Annals* 33:211-321.

1109. Turner, A.
1984 Behavioral Inferences Based on Frequencies in Bone Assemblages from Archaeological Sites. In *Frontiers: Southern African Archaeology Today*, edited by M. Hall, G. Avery, D.M. Avery, M.L. Wilson, and A.J.B. Humphreys, pp. 363-366. British Archaeological Reports, BAR International Series No. 207. Oxford.

1110. Turner, A.
1984 Identifying Bone-accumulating Agents. In *Frontiers: Southern African Archaeology Today*, edited by M. Hall, G. Avery, D.M. Avery, M.L. Wilson, and A.J.B. Humphreys, pp. 334-339. British Archaeological Reports, BAR International Series No. 207. Oxford.

1111. Turner, C.G.
    1983 Taphonomic Reconstruction of Human Violence and Cannibalism Based on Mass Burials in the American Southwest. In *Carnivores, Human Scavengers and Predators*, edited by G.M. LeMoine and A.S. MacEachern, pp. 219-240. (15th Annual Chacmool Conference, Proceedings). Archaeological Association, Department of Archaeology, University of Calgary, Alberta.
1112. Turner, C.G., and N.T. Morris
    1970 A Massacre at Hopi. *American Antiquity* 35:320-331.
1113. Ubelaker, D.H.
    1974 Reconstruction of Demographic Profiles from Ossuary Skeletal Samples. *Smithsonian Contributions to Anthropology* No. 18. Washington, D.C.
1114. Uerpmann, H.-P.
    1978 The "KNOCOD" System for Processing Data on Animal Bones from Archaeological Sites. *Peabody Museum of Archaeology and Ethnology. Bulletin* 2:149-167.
1115. Valentine, J.W., and R.G. Peddicord
    1967 Evaluation of Fossil Assemblages by Cluster Analysis. *Journal of Paleontology* 41:502-507.
1116. Valoch, K.
    1982 Die Beingeräte von Predmostí in Mähren (Tschechoslowakei). (The Bone Tools from Predmosti in Moravia, Czechoslovakia; in German with English abstract). *Anthropologie* 20:57-69.
1117. Van Couvering, J.A.H.
    1980 Community Evolution in East Africa During the Late Cenozoic. In *Fossils in the Making: Vertebrate Taphonomy and Paleoecology*, edited by A.K. Behrensmeyer and A.P. Hill, pp. 272-298. University of Chicago Press, Chicago.
1118. Van Der Lingen, G.J., and P.B. Andrews
    1969 Hoof-print Structures in Beach Sand. *Journal of Sedimentary Petrology* 39:350-357.
1119. Van Der Merwe, N.J.
    1987 Comment on Blumenschine 1987, with reply. *Current Anthropology* 28:400.
1120. Vaughan, J.
    1975 *The Physiology of Bone*. 2nd ed. Clarendon Press, Oxford.
1121. Vehik, S.C.
    1977 Bone Fragments and Bone Grease Manufacturing: A Review of Their Archaeological Use and Potential. *Plains Anthropologist* 22:169-182.
1122. Verbicky-Todd, E.
    1984 *Communal Buffalo Hunting Among the Plains Indians*. Alberta Archaeological Survey. Occasional Paper No. 24.
1123. Vereshchagin, N.K.
    1951 Circumstances of Mass Mortality and of Fossil Deposition of Terrestrial Vertebrates in Transcaucana (in Russian). *Zoologicheskii Zhurnal* 30:616-619.
1124. Vereshchagin, N.K.
    1961 On the Typology of Burial Places of the Remains of Terrestrial Vertebrates in Quaternary Deposits (in Russian). In *Materialy Vsesoiuznogo Soveshchaniia*, vol. 1, edited by E.V. Shantser, pp. 377-387. (Vsesiuznoe Soveshchanie po Izucheniiu Chetvertichnogo Perioda, Moscow, 1957). Akademiia Nauk SSSR, Moscow. Otdelenie Geologo-Geograficheskikh Nauk.
1125. Vereshchagin, N.K.
    1967 Primitive Hunters and Pleistocene Extinction in the Soviet Union. In *Pleistocene Extinctions*, edited by P.S. Martin and H.E. Wright, pp. 365-398. Yale University Press, New Haven.
1126. Verzilin, N.N., and L.A. Nesov
    1978 Ob Usloviykh Sushchestvovaniya Reltilii Mela Fergahy i Nekotorykh Tafonomichskikh Zakonomernostyakh Zakhoroneniya ikh Ostatkov (On the Conditions for the Occurrence of Cretaceous Reptiles of Fergana and some Taphonomic Principles of the Burial of Their Remains; in Russian). In *Voprosy Tafonomii i Paleobiologii*, Chaired by B.S. Soklov, pp. 56-65. SSSR, Akademiya Nauk, Vsesoyuznoe Paleontologicheskoe Obshchestvo. Trudy Sessi 20. Leningrad.
1127. Veyrier, M., and J. Combier
    1952 L'Industrie Osseuse Mousterienne de la Grotte Neron a Soyons (Ardeche). *Anthropologie* 56:383-385.
1128. Visher, G.S.
    1965 Fluvial Processes as Interpreted from Ancient and Recent Fluvial Deposits. In *Primary Sedimentary Structures and Their Hydrodynamic Interpretation*, edited by G. V. Middleton, pp. 116-132. Society of Economic Paleontologists and Mineralogists. Special Publications No. 12.
1129. Voigt, E.
    1984 Iron Age Faunal Analysis--Problems and Possibilities. In *Frontiers: Southern African Archaeology Today*, edited by M. Hall, G. Avery, D.M. Avery, M.L. Wilson, and A.J.B. Humphreys, pp. 352-356. British Archaeological Reports, BAR International Series No. 207. Oxford.
1130. Von Endt, D.W., and D.J. Ortner
    1984 Experimental Effects of Bone Size and Temperature on Bone Diagenesis. *Journal of Archaeological Sciences* 11:247-253.
1131. Voorhies, M.R.
    1969 *Taphonomy and Population Dynamics of an Early Pliocene Vertebrate Fauna, Knox County, Nebraska*. Contributions to Geology. University of Wyoming, Laramie. Special Papers No. 1
1132. Voorhies, M.R.
    1969 Sampling Difficulties in Reconstructing Late Tertiary Mammalian Communities. In *Proceedings of the 6th North American Paleontological Convention* pp. 454-468.
1133. Vrba, E.S.
    1976 *The Fossil Bovidae of Sterkfontein, Swartkraus and Kromdraai*. Transvaal Museum, Pretoria. Memoirs No. 21.

1134. Vrba, E.S.
1980 The Significance of Bovid Remains as Indications of Environment and Predation Patterns. In *Fossils in the Making: Vertebrate Taphonomy and Paleoecology*, edited by A.K. Behrensmeyer and A.P. Hill, pp. 247-271. University of Chicago Press.

1135. Vrba, E.S.
1981 The Kromdraai Australopithecine Site Revisited in 1980: Recent Investigations and Results. *Transvaal Museum, Pretoria. Annals* 33:17-60.

1136. Wadell, H.
1932 Volume, Shape, and Roundness of Rock Particles. *Journal of Geology* 40:443-451.

1137. Walker, A.C.
1980 Functional Anatomy and Taphonomy. In *Fossils in the Making: Vertebrate Taphonomy and Paleoecology*, edited by A.K. Behrensmeyer and A.P. Hill, pp. 182-196. University of Chicago Press, Chicago.

1138. Walker, K.R.
1972 Trophic Analysis: A Method for Studying the Function of Ancient Communities. *Journal of Paleontology* 46:82-93.

1139. Walker, K.R., and L.P. Alberstadt
1975 Ecological Succession as an Aspect of Structure in Fossil Communities. *Paleobiology* 1:238-257.

1140. Walker, P.L., and J.C. Long
1977 An Experimental Study of the Morphological Characteristics of Tool Marks. *American Antiquity* 42:605-616.

1141. Walters, I.
1984 Gone to the Dogs: A Study of Bone Attrition at a Central Australian Campsite. *Mankind* 14:389-400.

1142. Walters, I.
1985 Bone Loss: One Explicit Quantitative Guess. *Current Anthropology* 26:642-643.

1143. Warme, J.E.
1969 Live and Dead Molluscs in a Coastal Lagoon. *Journal of Paleontology* 43:141-150.

1144. Washburn, S.L.
1957 Australopithecines: The Hunters or the Hunted? *American Anthropologist* 59:612-614.

1145. Wasmund, E.
1926 Biocoenose und Thantocoenose. *Archiv für Hydrobiologie*, New Series, 17:1-116.

1146. Watkins, L.L., and W.M. Bass
1982 Spring and Summer Decay Rates in Knoxville, Tennessee. Program of 34th Annual Meeting of the American Academy of Forensic Sciences, Colorado Springs, Colorado, pp. 98-99.

1147. Watson, G.S.
1966 The Statistics of Orientation Data. *Journal of Geology* 74:786-797.

1148. Watson, J.P.N.
1972 Fragmentation Analysis of Animal Bone Samples from Archaeological Sites. *Archaeometry* 14:221-228.

1149. Weigelt, J.
1927 *Rezente Wirbeltierleichen und ihre Paläobiologische Bedeutung*. Max Weg, Leipzig.

1150. Weigelt, J.
1935 Some Remarks on the Excavations in the Geisel Valley. *Research and Progress* 1:155-159.

1151. Welbourne, R.G.
1975 Tautswe Iron Age Site: Its Yield of Bones. *Botswana Notes and Records* 7:1-16.

1152. Wells, C.
1960 A Study of Cremation. *Antiquity* 34:29-37.

1153. Wells, C.
1967 Pseudopathology. In *Diseases in Antiquity*, edited by D. Brothwell and A.T. Sandison, pp. 5-19. C.C. Thomas, Springfield, Ill.

1154. Wells, L.H.
1973 Baboons Sheltering in Caves. *South African Journal of Science* 69:279.

1155. Wessen, G., F.H. Ruddy, C.E. Gustafson, and H. Irwin
1977 Characterization of Archaeological Bone by Neutron Activation Analysis. *Archaeometry* 19:200-205.

1156. Western, D.
1971 Giraffe Chewing a Grant's Gazelle Carcass. *East African Wildlife Journal* 9:156-157.

1157. Western, D.
1980 Linking the Ecology of Past and Present Mammal Communities. In *Fossils in the Making: Vertebrate Taphonomy and Paleoecology*, edited by A.K. Behrensmeyer and A.P. Hill, pp. 41-54. University of Chicago Press, Chicago.

1158. Wheat, J.B.
1972 *The Olsen-Chubbuck Site: A Paleo-Indian Bison Kill*. Society for American Archaeology. Memoir No. 26.

1159. Wheat, J.B.
1979 *The Jurgens Site*. Plains Anthropologist. Memoir No. 15.

1160. Wheat, J.B.
1982 Bone Technology at Jurgens, Olsen-Chubbuck and Little Box Elder. *Canadian Journal of Anthropology* 2:169-177.

1161. White, E.M., and L.A. Hannus
1983 Chemical Weathering of Bone in Archaeological Soils. *American Antiquity* 48:316-322.

1162. White, R.
1982 Rethinking the Middle/Upper Paleolithic Transition. *Current Anthropology* 23:169-192.

1163. White, S.E.
1976 Is Frost Action Really Only Hydration Shattering?: A Review. *Arctic and Alpine Research* 8:1-6.

1164. White, T.D.
1985 Acheulian Man in Ethiopia's Middle Awash Valley: the Implications of Cutmarks on the Bodo Cranium. 8th Kroon Lecture, Stichting Nederlands Museum voor Anthropologie en Praeshisorie, Amsterdam, 19 April 1982.

1165. White, T.D.
1986 Cutmarks on the Bodo Cranium: A Case of Prehistoric Defleshing. *American Journal of Physical Anthropology* 69:503-509.

1166. White, T.E.
   1952 Observations on the Butchering Technique of Some Aboriginal Peoples, No. 1. *American Antiquity* 17:337-338.
1167. White, T.E.
   1953 Observations on the Butchering Technique of Some Aboriginal Peoples, No. 2. *American Antiquity* 19:160-164.
1168. White, T.E.
   1954 Observations on the Butchering Technique of Some Aboriginal Peoples, Nos. 3, 4, 5, 6. *American Antiquity* 19:254-264.
1169. White, T.E.
   1955 Observations on the Butchering Technique of Some Aboriginal Peoples, Nos. 7, 8, 9. *American Antiquity* 21:170-178.
1170. Wild, C.J., and R.K. Nichol
   1983 Estimation of the Original Number of Individuals from Paired Bone Counts Using Estimates of the Krantz Type. *Journal of Field Archaeology* 10:337-344.
1171. Wilkinson, P.F.
   1976 "Random" Hunting and the Composition of Faunal Samples from Archaeological Excavations: A Modern Example from New Zealand. *Journal of Archaeological Science* 3:321-328.
1172. Will, R.T.
   1982 Review of *Bones*, by L.R. Binford. *Zooarchaeological Research News* 1:7-8.
1173. Willis, D.G.
   1977 A Kinematic Model of Preferred Orientation. *Geological Society of America. Bulletin* 88:883-894.
1174. Wilmeth, R.
   1977 Pit-House Construction and the Disturbance of Stratified Sites. *Canadian Journal of Archaeology* 1:135-140.
1175. Wilson, M.C.
   1982 Cut Marks and Early Hominids: Evidence for Skinning. *Nature* 298:303.
1176. Wilson, M.C.
   1983 Canid Scavengers and Butchering Patterns: Evidence from a 3600 Year Old Bison Bone Bed in Alberta. In *Carnivores, Human Scavengers and Predators*, edited by G.M. LeMoine and A.S. MacEachern, pp. 94-139. (15th Annual Chacmool Conference, Proceedings). Archaeological Association, Department of Archaeology, University of Calgary, Alberta.
1177. Wilson, V.J.
   1969 The Large Mammals of the Matopos National Park. *Arnoldia* 4(13):1-32.
1178. Wing, S.L., and L.J. Hickey
   1982 Time Scales in Megafloral Assemblages (Abstract). *Journal of Paleontology* 56(Supp. No. 2):30.
1179. Witter, D.C.
   1974 Nunamiut Caribou Processing, Categories of Faunal Analysis, and Organizational Measures of Subsistence Strategy. Paper presented at the annual meeting of the Society for American Archaeology, Washington, D.C.

1180. Wolberg, D.L.
   1970 The Hypothesized Osteodontokeratic Culture of the *Australopithecinae*: A Look at the Evidence: The Opinions. *Current Anthropology* 11:23-27.
1181. Wolberg, D.L.
   1984 Book Review of: *Taphonomy and Paleoecology of the Christensen Bog*. (By R.W. Graham, J.A. Holman, and P.W. Parmalee). *Journal of Vertebrate Paleontology* 3:232-233.
1182. Wolff, R.G.
   1973 Hydrodynamic Sorting and Ecology of a Pleistocene Mammalian Assemblage from California (U.S.A.). *Palaeogeography, Palaeoclimatology, Palaeoecology* 13:91-101.
1183. Wolff, R.G.
   1975 Sampling and Sample Size in Ecological Analyses of Fossil Mammals. *Paleobiology* 1:195-204.
1184. Wolpoff, M.H.
   1986 More on Zhoukoudian (Comment on Binford and Ho 1985). *Current Anthropology* 27:46-45.
1185. Wood, A.E.
   1952 Tooth-Marks on Bones of the Orleton Farms Mastodon. *Ohio Journal of Science* 52:27-28.
1186. Wood, W.R.
   1962 Notes on the Bison Bone from the Paul Brave, Huff, and Demery Sites (Oahe Reservoir). *Plains Anthropologist* 7:201-204.
1187. Wood, W.R.
   1968 Mississippian Hunting and Butchering Patterns: Bone from the Vista Shelter, 23SR-20, Missouri. *American Antiquity* 33:170-179.
1188. Wood, W.R., and D.L. Johnson
   1978 A Survey of Disturbance Processes in Archaeological Site Formation. In *Advances in Archaeological Method and Theory*, vol. 1, edited by M.B. Schiffer, pp. 315-381. Academic Press, New York.
1189. Woodward, G.D., and L.F. Marcus
   1973 Rancho La Brea Fossil Deposits: A Re-Evaluation from Stratigraphic and Geological Evidence. *Journal of Paleontology* 47:54-69.
1190. Wright, T., and L.S. Kornicker
   1962 Inland Transport of Marine Shells by Birds on Perez Island, Alacran Reef, Campeche Bank, Mexico. *Journal of Geology* 70:616-618.
1191. Wyatt, J.R.
   1971 Osteophagia in Masai Giraffe. *East African Wildlife Journal* 9:157.
1192. Wycoff, R.W.G.
   1972 *The Biochemistry of Animal Fossils*. Scientechnica, Bristol.
1193. Wyckoff, R.W.G., and A.R. Doberenz
   1965 The Electron Microscopy of Rancho La Brea Bone. *National Academy of Sciences, Washington, D.C. Proceedings* 53:230-233.
1194. Wyckoff, R.W.G., and A.R. Doberenz
   1965 Le Collagène dans les Dents Pléistocènes. *Journal de Microscopie* 4:271-274.

1195. Wyckoff, R.W.G, E. Wagner, P. Matter III, and A.R. Doberenz
    1963 Collagen in Fossil Bone. *National Academy of Sciences, Washington D.C. Proceedings* 50:215-218. Washington, DC.
1196. Wymer, J.J.
    1986 Comment on Bunn and Kroll 1986. *Current Anthropology* 27:447-448.
1197. Yaalon, D.H., and D. Kalmar
    1978 Dynamics of Cracking and Swelling Clay Soils: Displacement of Skeletal Grains, Optimum Depth of Slickensides, and Rate of Intra-Pedonic Turbation. *Earth Surface Processes* 3:31-42.
1198. Yacobaccio, H.D.
    1985 Comment on Binford and Ho 1985 (Reply by Binford and Ho). *Current Anthropology* 26:436.
1199. Yanin, B.T.
    1978 Iskopaemye Sledy Zhiznedeyatelnosti Organizmov v Melovykh i Paleogenovykh Otlozheniyakh Kryma (Fossil Tracks of Living Organisms in Cretaceous and Paleogene Deposits of the Crimea; in Russian). In *Voprosy Tafonomii i Paleobiologii*, Chaired by B.S. Soklov, pp. 173-185. SSSR, Akademiya Nauk, Vsesoyuznoe Paleontologicheskoe Obshchestvo. Trudy Sessi 20. Leningrad.
1200. Yanin, B.T.
    1978 Perenos i Pereotlozhenie Ostatkov Organiemov (The Transport and Redeposition of the Remains of Organisms; in Russian). In *Voprosy Tafonomii i Paleobiologii*, Chaired by B.S. Soklov, pp. 185-193. SSSR, Akademiya Nauk, Vsesoyuznoe Paleontologicheskoe Obshchestvo. Trudy Sessi 20. Leningrad.
1201. Yellen, J.E.
    1977 Cultural Patterning in Faunal Remains: Evidence from the !Kung Bushmen. In *Experimental Archaeology*, edited by D. Ingersoll, J.E. Yellen, and W. MacDonald, pp. 271-331. Columbia University Press, New York.
1202. Yesner, D.R.
    1980 Caribou Exploitation in Interior Alaska: Paleoecology of Two Paxson Lake Sites. *University of Alaska. Anthropological Papers* 19(2):15-32.
1203. Yesner, D.R., and R. Bonnichsen
    1979 Caribou Metapodial Shaft Splinter Technology. *Journal of Archaeological Science* 6:303-308.
1204. Yi, S.
    1985 Comment on Binford and Ho 1985 (Reply by Binford and Ho). *Current Anthropology* 26:436.
1205. Yochelson, E.L., D. Dockery, and H. Wolf
    1983 *Predation on Sub-Holocene Scaphopod Mollusks from Southern Louisiana*. U.S. Geological Survey. Professional Paper 1282.
1206. You, Y.-Z.
    1986 Comment on Binford and Stone 1986. *Current Anthropology* 27:471.
1207. Young, D.E.
    1989 How Powerful are Archaeological Inferences Based Upon Experimental Replication? In *Bone Modification*, edited by R. Bonnichsen and M. Sorg (1st International Bone Modification Conference, Proceedings). Center for the Study of the First Americans, Orono, Maine.
1208. Zach, R.
    1967 Selection and Dropping of Whelks by Northwestern Crows. *Behaviour* 67:134-148.
1209. Zangerl, R.
    1969 On the Geologic Significance of Perfectly Preserved Fossils. *Proceedings of the 6th North American Paleontological Convention*, pp. 1207-1222.
1210. Zangerl, R., B.G. Woodland, E.S. Richardson, and D.L. Zachry
    1969 Early Diagenetic Phenomena in the Fayetteville Black Shale (Mississippian) of Arkansas. *Sedimentary Geology* 3:87-119.
1211. Zapfe, H.
    1981 Ein Schädel von *Mesopithecus* mit Biss-Spuren. (A Skull of *Mesopithecus* with Bite Marks). *Folia Primatologica* 35:248-258. (English Abstract).
1212. Zarkhidze, V.S., and L.A. Tverskaya
    1978 Zakonomernosti Prostessa Zakhoroneniya Morskiky Organiemov v Svyazi s Paleoekologicheskimi Usloviyami ikh Obitaniya v Noveishee Vremya a Severnykh Raionakh Timano-Uralskoi Oblasti (The Burial of Marine Orgainisms as Related to Their Discovery at Another Time in the Northern Regions of the Timan-Uralian Area; in Russian). In *Voprosy Tafonomii i Paleobiologii*, Chaired by B.S. Soklov, pp. 75-81. SSSR, Akademiya Nauk, Vsesoyuznoe Paleontologicheskoe Obshchestvo. Trudy Sessi 20. Leningrad.
1213. Zegwaard, G.
    1959 Headhunting Practices of the Asmat of Netherlands New Giunea. *American Anthropologist* 61:1020-1041.
1214. Ziegler, A.C.
    1973 *Inference from Prehistoric Faunal Remains*. Addison-Wesley Module in Anthropology No. 43. Addison-Wesley, Reading, Massachusetts.
1215. Zierhut, N.W.
    1967 Bone Breaking Activities of the Calling Lake Cree. *Alberta Anthropologist* 1:33-36.
1216. Zimmerman, M.R., and R.H. Tedford
    1976 Histologic Structures Preserved for 21,300 Years. *Science* 194:183-184.

Author Index

Abbie, A.A., 1
Adams, J., 2
Agenbroad, L.D., 4
Ager, D.V., 3
Agogino, G.A., 5
Aguirre, E., 91
Aigner, J.S., 6, 7
Aigner, T., 8
Akopyan, M.M., 9
Alberstadt, L.P., 1139
Albertson, M.L., 1031
Alcock, J., 610
Alexander, A.K., 10
Alexandersson, E.T., 11, 12
Aliev, F.F., 13
Alimen, M.H., 14
Aliyev, O.B., 15
Aliyev, R.A., 16
Allen, J., 17, 606
Allen, J.R.L., 18, 19, 20
Allison, H.J., 216, 217, 218
Alvis, L.A., 790
Ambrose, S.H., 21
Anderson, C.M., 22
Anderson, J.L., 23
Anderson, S., 24
Andrews, P., 25, 26, 27, 28
Andrews, P.B., 1118
Anonymous, 29
Antia, D.D.J., 30
Appleby, R.M., 31
Archer, M., 32, 33
Arens, W., 34
Armelagos, G.J., 910
Arnold, A.J., 35
Arnold, C.A., 36
Ascenzi, A., 37
Atkinson, R.J.C., 38
Avery, D.M., 39
Avery, G., 40, 41

Bachinskii, G.A., 42
Bacskai, J.A., 219, 479, 480, 481
Badgley, C.E., 43
Bagnold, R.A., 44, 45
Bailey, J.W., 46, 47
Baker, C.M., 48
Baker, R.T., 336
Baker, V.R., 49, 50
Banks, E.E., 51
Baranov, V.N., 52
Barash, D.P., 53
Barbour, E.H., 54
Barbour, E.P., 55
Barnhardt, M.L., 598
Barnosky, A.D., 56
Barondess, D.R., 311
Barral, L., 177
Bass, W.M., 451, 941, 942, 1146
Bathurst, R.G.C., 57
Bayer, U., 58
Baynes, A., 59
Bearder, S.K., 60
Beck, L.A., 61
Becker, H., 113
Beebe, B.F., 62, 610
Beerbower, J.R., 63
Begouen, C., 64, 840
Begouen, L., 64, 840
Behrensmeyer, A.K., 65, 66, 67, 68, 69, 70, 71, 72, 73, 74, 75, 76, 77, 78, 79, 80, 81, 82, 83, 84, 124, 206, 336, 438, 545, 546, 547, 683
Beinhart, G., 868
Bently, D., 956
Bentzen, R., 85
Berg, S., 86
Berger, J., 87
Berner, R.A., 88
Bertram, J.B., 106
Betancourt, J.L., 89
Beuge, L.J., 560
Biberson, P., 90, 91

Biddick, K.A., 92
Binford, L.R., 93, 94, 95, 96, 97, 98, 99, 100, 101, 102, 103, 104, 105, 106, 107, 108, 109, 110, 111, 112
Bird, F., 113
Bird, R.D., 114
Bishop, W.W., 115
Black, D., 116
Blakely, R.L., 189
Blatt, H., 117
Blodgett, R.H., 353
Blumenschine, R.J., 118, 119, 120, 121, 122, 205
Boaz, N.T., 123, 124, 588
Boeck, B., 125
Boggs, S., Jr., 250
Bokonyi, S., 126
Bonfield, W., 127, 128, 129
Bonnichsen, R., 130, 131, 132, 133, 134, 135, 136, 137, 138, 139, 140, 141, 142, 501, 646, 808, 1053, 1094, 1203
Bonucci, E., 143
Bornemissza, G.F., 144
Borrero, L.A., 145
Bosler, W., 1012, 1013, 1014
Bottjer, D.J., 982
Boucot, A.J., 146, 147, 778
Bown, T.M., 148, 149, 353
Boyd, D.W., 150
Boyde, A., 183
Boyer, P., 151
Brace, W., 147
Brain, C.K., 152, 153, 154, 155, 156, 157, 158, 159, 160, 161, 162, 163, 164, 165, 166, 167, 168, 169, 170
Brajnikov, B., 219, 479
Brézillon, M., 699
Breder, C.M., 171
Brenchley, P.J., 172
Brenner, K., 987
Brett, D.W., 947
Breuil, H.A., 173, 174, 175, 176, 177, 178
Bridge, J.S., 179
Brink, J., 180
Brink, J.S., 181
Bromage, T.G., 182, 183
Bromley, R.G., 184
Brongersma-Sanders, M., 185
Brooks, R.H., 186
Brooks, S.T., 265
Brothwell, D.R., 187, 188
Brown, A.B., 189
Brown, K.A., 860
Brown, P., 190
Brown, R.J., 649
Brown, S.O., 373, 374
Brumley, J.H., 191
Bryan, A.L., 192, 193
Bryant, L.A., 481
Buckland, W., 194
Buczko, C.M., 195
Buikstra, J.E., 196, 464, 680
Bunn, H.T., 197, 198, 199, 200, 201, 202, 203, 204, 205, 206, 207, 208

Buntley, G.J., 209
Burnstein, A.H., 210
Burt, T.P., 211
Buskirk, S.W., 212
Butler, P.R., 213

Cadee, G.C., 214
Cahen, D., 215
Camp, C.L., 216, 217, 218, 219, 220, 221, 222, 223
Campbell, J.B., 224
Camps-Fabrer, H., 225
Canby, T.Y., 226
Carlson, D.L., 1054
Carnot, A., 227
Caro, T.M., 121
Carver, R.E., 228
Case, E.C., 229
Casteel, R.W., 230, 231, 232, 233, 234, 235
Caughley, G., 236
Cerutti, R.A., 321
Chaplin, R.E., 237
Chapman, R.F., 238
Chave, K.E., 239, 240, 241
Cheng, T.-K., 242
Chenoweth, P.A., 243
Chisholm, B.S., 244
Churcher, C.S., 622
Clark, J., 245
Clark, J.D., 246
Clark, W.E.L., 247
Clarke, R.J., 248
Clason, A.T., 249
Clifton, H.E., 250
Clutton-Brock, J., 251
Coe, M., 252, 253
Cole, G.H., 254, 255, 557
Cole, J.E., 256
Collett, M.H., 746
Collings, H.D., 1068
Combier, J., 1127
Cones, H.R., 257
Conkey, M.W., 258
Converse, H.H., 259
Conybeare, A., 260
Cook, H., 702
Cook, J., 26, 261, 262
Cook, S.F., 263, 264, 265
Cooke, H.B.S., 77
Corbett, M.E., 401
Corfield, T.F., 266
Cornaby, B.W., 267
Corner, G., 817
Cornwall, I.W., 268
Corte, A.E., 269
Corydon, S.C., 270
Crader, D.C., 271, 272, 273, 274, 439, 582
Crawford, I.M., 33
Crick, R.E., 275, 916
Cring, D., 360
Cruxent, J.M., 193, 953

Cruz-Uribe, K., 276, 643
Cuffey, R.J., 277
Currey, J.D., 210, 278, 583
Curry, J.D., 745
Curtis, J.D., 279

D'Andrea, C.A., 280, 610
Daeschler, E., 972
Dailey, R.C., 281
Dallman, J.E., 282
Daly, P., 880
Damrosch, D.B., 445
Damrosch, D.R., 445
Damuth, J., 283
Dapples, E.C., 284
Dart, R.A., 285, 286, 287, 288, 289, 290, 291, 292, 293, 294, 295, 296, 297, 298, 299, 300, 301, 302, 303, 304, 305, 306, 759
Darwin, C.R., 307
Das, S.K., 308, 309
Davidson, F.D., 310
Davis, D.D., 311
Davis, K.L., 1012, 1013, 1014
Davis, O.K., 89
Davis, S., 1040
De Ploey, J., 312, 313, 314
De Vis, C.W., 315, 316, 317
Dechant-Boaz, D.E., 83, 318, 319
Dechant, D.E. (*See also* Dechant-Boaz, D.E.), 78
Deevey, E.S., 320
Deffeyes, K.S., 241
DeMar, R., 147
Demere, T.A., 321
Dence, W.A., 322
Dibble, D.S., 323
Dietz, E.F., 324
Dincauze, D.F., 325
Dixon, E.J., 326, 327
Doberenz, A.R., 309, 328, 329, 330, 384, 1193, 1194, 1195
Dockery, D., 1205
Dodd, J.R., 331
Dodds, D.G., 332
Dodson, P., 333, 334, 335, 336, 337
Domenech, R., 756
Donohue, J., 948
Donovan, P., 53
Doroshenko, A.A., 854
Dortch, C.E., 338, 339, 340, 341, 342
Douglas-Hamilton, I., 344, 345
Douglas-Hamilton, O., 345
Douglas, A.M., 343
Driesch, A. von den, 346
Driscoll, E.G., 347, 348
Driver, J.C., 349, 350, 351
Dubiel, R.F., 352, 353
Dubois, E., 354
Duckworth, W.L.H., 355
Ducos, P., 356
Duke, G.E., 357, 358
Dummond, D.E., 359

Dunbar, J.S., 360
Durham, J.W., 361
Dwyer, D.P., 1047

Eastoe, B., 362
Eastoe, J.E., 362
Edinger, T., 949
Efremov, I.A., 363, 364, 365, 366, 367
Einarsen, A.S., 368
Ekland, C., 470
Elder, R.L., 369
Eloff, F.C., 370, 371
Emlem, J.T., Jr., 380
Emmett, W.W., 698
Enlow, D.H., 372, 373, 374
Ericson, J.E., 375
Ericson, Per G.P., 376
Erlandson, J.M., 377
Estes, R.D., 990
Evans, A.C., 378
Evans, E.M.N., 379
Evans, F.C., 380
Evans, F.G., 381, 382, 383
Evans, J., 615
Evanson, O.A., 357, 358
Evers, T.M., 750
Everts, J.M., 384
Ewer, R.F., 385, 386
Ezra-Cohn, H., 265

Fagerstrom, J.A., 387
Fahnestock, R.K., 388, 502
Falk, C.R., 389
Faufman, D., 420
Fay, F.H., 390
Fichter, E., 391
Fieller, N.R.J., 392
Fiorillo, A.R., 393
Fisher, D.C., 394, 395, 396, 397, 398, 1015
Fisunenko, O.P., 399
Fleming, R.L., 400
Flinn, R.M., 401
Floyd, T.J., 402
Foley, R., 403, 404
Folk, R.L., 105
Forbes, G., 406
Forbis, R.G., 407
Foster, G., 1016
Frankel, V.H., 210
Frankforter, W.O., 5
Freeman, L.G., 408, 409
Frison, G.C., 410, 411, 412, 413, 414, 415, 416, 417, 418, 419
Fürsich, F.T., 421, 422
Fuchs, C., 420
Fulton, C., 219
Futterer, E., 423

Gabriel, D., 719
Galdikas, B.M.F., 424, 425
Garrels, R.M., 241

Gashwilder, J.S., 426
Gautier, A., 427, 428
Gavrilishin, V.I., 429
Gebo, D.L., 430
Gekker, R.F., 431
Gentry, A.W., 432
Gifford-Gonzalez, D.P., 441, 442, 443, 444, 445, 446
Gifford, D.P. (*See also* Gifford-Gonzalez, D.P.), 433, 434, 435, 436, 437, 438, 439, 440
Gilbert, A.S., 447, 448, 449
Gilbert, B.M., 450, 451
Gill, E.D., 452, 453
Ginda, V.A., 454
Gladfelter, B.G., 455
Gladkih, M.I., 456
Glimcher, M.J., 457
Glover, E.C., 458
Glover, P.E., 458
Glue, D.E., 459
Goldberg, P., 460
Goodard, C.B., 461
Gordon, B.C., 463
Gordon, C.C., 464
Gordon, K.D., 79, 84
Goretskiy, V.A., 462
Gottelli, M.D., 1028
Gotthardt, R.M., 280
Gould, R.A., 465
Gow, C.E., 466
Gradzinski, R., 467
Graham, A.D., 468
Graham, R.W., 469
Granger, W., 1035
Grant, P., 470
Grassé, P-P., 471
Gratacap, L.P., 472
Grayson, D.K., 235, 473, 474, 475, 476, 477
Graziani, G., 143
Green, M., 222, 223
Green, R.H., 478
Gregory, J.T., 80, 479, 480, 481
Grigson, C., 482
Grinnell, J., 483
Grobler, J.H., 484
Gronnøw, B., 485
Grossman, J.D., 1037
Gruhn, R., 193
Gubser, N.J., 486
Guilday, J.E., 487, 488
Gunn, A., 489
Gunter, G., 490
Gustafson, C.E., 956, 1155
Guthrie, R.D., 491, 492, 493, 494
Guthrie, R.D., 1086
Gutschick, R.C., 940
Guy, J.B.M., 17

Habe, T., 797
Hagdorn, H., 8
Hall, S.L., 495

Hampel, J., 123
Hannus, L.A., 496
Hannus, L.A., 1161
Hansen, K.L., 590
Hanson, C.B., 80, 497
Happold, D.C.D., 498
Happold, M., 498
Hare, P.E., 499
Harger, J.H., 560
Harington, C.R., 500, 501
Harms, J.C., 502
Harris, K.J.W.K., 206
Harris, R.S., 308
Harrison, T., 503
Hartzell, J.C., 504
Hattin, D.E., 277
Haushild, W.L., 388
Hay, O.P., 505, 506
Haynes, C.V., 591
Haynes, G.A., 260, 507, 508, 509, 510, 511, 512, 513, 514, 515, 516, 517, 914
Healer, J., 113
Hecker, R.F. (*See* Gekker, R.F.), 431
Heizer, R.F., 264, 518, 519
Henderson, P., 520
Hendey, Q.B., 521
Hendricks, S.B., 522
Hendy, B.Q., 571
Henschel, J.R., 523
Henschel, J.R., 523, 1088
Henshaw, J., 524
Herm, D., 525
Herrmann, B., 526
Herrmann, G., 527
Hewson, R., 528, 529
Hickey, L.J., 1178
High, L.R., Jr., 884
Hill, A.P., 530, 531, 532, 533, 534, 535, 536, 537, 538, 539, 540, 541, 542, 543, 544, 545, 546, 547, 548
Hill, W.L., 522
Hillefors, Å., 549
Hillman, A.K.K., 550
Hillman, J.C., 550
Ho, C.K., 107
Hobson, K.A., 244
Hofman, J.L., 551
Hogg, G., 552
Holman, J.A., 469
Holtzman, R.C., 553
Hooker, P.J., 1023
Horton, D.R., 554, 555
Houston, R.S., 556
Howell, F.C., 557
Hrdlicka, A., 558
Hudson, G.E., 615
Hudson, J.D., 559
Huelke, D.F., 560
Hughes, A.R., 561, 562, 563, 564
Hughes, P.J., 565
Hunt, R.M., 566, 567

Ikawa-Smith, F., 568, 569
Ilani, G., 1040, 1041
Inazumi, A., 1069
Ingall, E., 907
Inglis, D.R., 570
Inskeep, R.R., 571
Iregren, E., 572
Irving, W.N., 573, 610
Irwin, H., 1155
Isaac, G.L., 206, 440, 446, 574, 575, 576, 577, 578, 579, 580, 581, 582
Isaacs, W.A., 583
Ivanov, A.N., 52

Jablonski, D., 625
Jackes, M., 584
Jackson, K.A., 585
Jacob, T., 586
Jafe, E.B., 587
Jegers, A.A., 357, 358
Johanson, D.C., 588
Johansson, C.E., 589
Johnson, D.L., 590, 591, 1188
Johnson, E., 592, 593, 594, 595, 596, 597
Johnson, L.J., 598
Johnson, M.D., 599
Johnson, R.G., 600, 601, 602
Jones, C.M., 603
Jones, G.L., 31
Jones, K.T., 604
Jones, P.R., 605
Jones, R., 606
Jonsson, R., 572
Jopling, A.V., 573, 607, 608, 609, 610, 863
Jordan, D., 63
Jordan, P.A., 402
Julig, P., 610

Kalmar, D., 1197
Karega-Munene, M., 611
Karplus, H., 612
Katsuta, T., 1069
Katzenburg, M.A., 613
Kauffman, E.G., 614
Kaufman, J., 567
Kaufulu, Z., 206
Keeley, H.C.M., 615
Kehoe, A.B., 618
Kehoe, T.F., 616, 617, 618
Keller, E.A., 619
Kelling, G., 620
Kelly, B.P., 390
Kelly, J.C., 556
Kendrick, G.W., 343
Kent, S., 621
Kenyon, W.A., 622
Kerfoot, W.C., 712
Kessler, A., 701
Khmelevskiy, Z.I., 462
Khozatskiy, L.I., 674

Kidder, T.R., 311
Kidwell, S.M., 81, 623, 624, 625
Kietzke, K.K., 245
Kindle, E.M., 626
King, E.W., 868, 869
Kirtsch-Armstrong, I., 573
Kitching, J.W., 306, 627, 628, 759
Klein, R.G., 276, 629, 630, 631, 632, 633, 634, 635, 636, 637, 638, 639, 640, 641, 642, 643, 979
Kleindienst, M.R., 557
Knyp, M., 244
Koch, C.P., 644, 645, 646
Koch, W., 647
Kolb, H.H., 529
Kolenosky, G.B., 891
Komar, P.D., 787
Konizeski, R.L., 648
Kontrovitz, M., 649
Konyushkov, K.N., 650
Korbel, A., 865
Kornicker, L.S., 1190
Kornietz, N.L., 456
Korschgen, L.J., 651
Korth, W.W., 652, 653
Kozicky, E.L., 279
Kozlowski, J.K., 654
Kozyar, L.A., 655
Krantz, G.S., 656
Kranz, P.M., 657, 658
Kraus, M.J., 148, 149
Krejci-Graf, V.K., 659
Kroll, E., 206
Kroll, E.M., 207, 208
Krumbein, W.C., 660, 661, 662, 663
Kruuk, H., 664, 665, 666, 667
Kühne, W.G., 673
Kubiak, H., 865
Kuenen, P.H., 668, 669, 670, 671, 672
Kulikov, M.V., 674
Kusmer, K., 675
Kuss, S.E., 676

LaBarbera, M., 677
Lafont, R., 678
Lakes, R., 679
Lambert, J.B., 680
Lampert, R.J., 565
Lanata, J.L., 681
Langbein, W.B., 682
Lantier, R., 178
Laporte, L.F., 683
Larson, D.W., 684
Lasker, H., 685
Lawrence, D.R., 686, 687
Laws, R.M., 468
Lawton, R.C., 688, 689
Leakey, L.S.B., 690
Leakey, M.D., 691
Ledger, J.A., 814
Leechman, D., 692

Lehman, J.P., 310
LeMort, F., 693, 959
Leopold, L.B., 682, 694, 695, 696, 697, 698
Leroi-Gourhan, A., 699
Lever, J., 700, 701, 702
Levine, M.A., 703
Levinson, M., 704
Lewin, R., 705
Lewy, Z., 706
Li, C.H., 128, 129
Liebowitz, H., 527
Lighthill, J.J., 707, 708
Lisowski, F.P., 709, 710
Little, K., 583
Llanos, G.A., 883
Loff, G., 358
Logan, A., 827
Long, C.A., 24, 712
Long, J.C., 1140
Loomis, F.B., 711
Lord, J.M., 28
Lorrain, D., 323
Losey, T.C., 713
Lü, Z., 714
Luchterhand, K., 715
Lund, R., 328
Lundelius, E.L., 716, 717
Lundy, J.K., 46, 47
Lupton, C., 718, 719
Lyman, R.L., 720, 721, 722, 723, 724, 725, 726, 727, 728, 729, 730, 731, 732, 733, 734, 735, 736, 737
Lyon, P.J., 738
Lyuleva, S.A., 739

MacDonald, D.W., 740, 741
MacDonald, K.B., 742
MacDonald, S.O., 212
MacGregor, A.G., 743, 744, 745
Maguire, J.M., 746
Maiklem, W.R., 747
Maltby, J.M., 748
Marcus, L.F., 1189
Marean, C.W., 749
Marker, M.E., 750
Marlow, C.A., 520
Marquina, M.J., 756
Marshall, F.B., 751, 752
Marshall, L., 753
Martin, H., 754
Martin, R., 755
Martinell, J., 756
Martinka, C.J., 757
Mason, R.J., 758, 759
Matsuy, V.M., 810
Matter, P., III, 1195
Matthews, J.M., 760
Matthews, J.V., 809
Mayhew, D.F., 761
Mbae, B.N., 762
McArdle, J.E., 763, 764, 924

McCarthy, B., 765
McCave, I.N., 787
McCormick, J.S., 766
McCullough, K.M., 767
McGinnis, H., 217
McGrew, P.O., 768, 769
McHenry, H.M., 770
McKee, E.D., 771
McKnight, D.G., 772
McLean, F.C., 773
McLeod, S.A., 815
Mead, E., 774
Mead, F.W., 869
Meadow, R.H., 775
Mech, L.D., 402, 776
Medway, L., 503
Meeks, S., 774
Meldgaard, M., 485
Melhorn, W.N., 619
Mellett, J.S., 777
Menard, H.W., 778
Mengoni Goñalons, G., 779
Mercier, M.L., 780
Merriam, J.C., 781
Merrilees, D., 33, 59, 341, 342, 343
Messer, M., 113
Meyer, G.E., 27
Mick, L.S., 108
Middleton, G.V., 117, 782
Miller, F.L., 489
Miller, G.J., 783, 784
Miller, G.S., 785
Miller, J.A., 1023
Miller, J.E., 786
Miller, J.P., 697
Miller, M.F., 330
Miller, M.C., 787
Miller, S.J., 788, 789, 791
Miller, W., 790
Mills, M.E.J., 793
Mills, M.G.L., 792, 793
Minikh, M.G., 794
Minnegal, M., 1047
Minnegal, M.M.A., 795, 796
Miyadi, D., 797
Moeyersons, J., 215, 314, 798
Mohl, U., 799
Molleson, T.I., 520
Montgomery, T.H., Jr., 800
Moon, E.L., 801
Morlan, R.E., 501, 802, 803, 804, 805, 806, 807, 808, 809, 1053
Morris, N.T., 1112
Morris, O.W., 426
Moskina, O.D., 810
Moss, C., 811
Mott, N.F., 812
Müller, A.H., 813
Muhs, D.R., 598
Mundlos, R., 8

Mundy, P.J., 814
Munson, P.J., 873
Munthe, K., 479, 815
Muravin, E.S., 52
Murie, O.J., 816
Murray, R., 117
Myers, T.P., 817
Myrick, R., 53
Myrick, R.M., 698

Nagle, J.S., 818, 819, 820
Nelson, C.M., 440, 446
Nelson, D.E., 244
Nelson, N.C., 821
Nesbit Evans, E.M., 28
Nesov, L.A., 1126
Neugebauer, J., 822
Neumann, T.W., 823
Newall, G., 172
Newcomer, M.H., 824
Newell, N.D., 150, 825
Nichol, R.K., 1170
Nichols, R.H., 217, 218, 219
Nickens, P.R., 826
Nielsen, B., 485
Noble, J.P.A., 827
Noe-Nygaard, N., 828, 829, 830, 831, 832, 833, 834, 835
Nordin, C.F., 1032
North, M.E.W., 836
Novak, I.D., 837
Nye, P.H., 838

O'Brien, C.J., 770
O'Brien, M.J., 737
Oakley, K.P., 839
Ochsenius, C., 193
Octobon, E., 840
Oldham, C., 841
Oliver, J.S., 842
Olsen, J.W., 843
Olsen, S.J., 844, 845
Olson, E.C., 846, 847, 848, 849
Ortner, D.J., 1130
Osgood, C., 850
Oshurkova, M.V., 851
Owens, D., 852
Owens, M.J., 852

Paine, G., 853
Papendick, R.I., 209
Papin, Yu.S., 854
Park, E., 855
Parker, R.B., 856, 857, 858
Parmalee, P.W., 469, 488
Parrish, W.C., 859
Pate, D., 860
Patrunov, D.K., 861
Paul, C.R.C., 862
Pavlish, L.A., 863, 864
Pawlicki, R., 865

Payne, A.G., 866
Payne, J.A., 867, 868, 869
Payne, S., 870, 871, 872, 873
Péwé, T.L., 883
Pearson, J., 874
Pearson, O.P., 875
Peddicord, R.G., 1115
Pei, G., 876
Pei, W.-C., 877, 878
Pemberton, D., 746
Perkins, D., 879, 880
Peske, G.R., 1077
Peterson, C.H., 881
Petit-Maire, N., 678
Pettijohn, F.J., 882, 900
Phillips-Conroy, J.E., 1019
Phillips, J.E. (See also Phillips-Conroy, J.E.), 1017, 1018
Picard, M.D., 884
Pideplichko, I.G., 885
Piekarski, K., 886
Piepenbrink, H., 887
Pierce, W.D., 888, 889, 890
Pilbeam, D.R., 27
Pimlott, D.H., 891
Piperno, D.R., 892
Pires-Ferreira, J.W., 923
Plug, I., 893, 894
Poggenpoel, C.A., 895
Poplin, F., 896, 897, 898, 899
Porter, J.K., 59
Potter, P.E., 900
Potts, R.B., 901, 902, 903, 904, 905, 906, 907
Pozorski, S., 908
Price, T.D., 909, 910
Prummel, W., 249
Pryor, J., 445
Putnam, F.W., 911

Raczynski, J., 912
Ragan, D.M., 913
Rancier, J., 914
Rapson, D.J., 915
Raup, D.M., 916, 917
Read-Martin, C.E., 919, 920, 921, 922
Read, C.E. (See also Read-Martin, C.E.), 918
Read, D.W., 920, 921, 922
Redding, R.W., 923, 924
Reed, B.P., 926
Reed, C.A., 925
Reed, C.I., 926
Reed, H.B., 927
Reher, C.A., 928
Reif, W.-E., 929, 930
Reilly, D.T., 210
Reineck, H.E., 931
Retallack, G.J., 932
Reynolds, T.E.G., 933
Richardson, E.S., 1210
Richardson, E.V., 1029, 1030, 1031, 1032
Richardson, P.R.K., 934

Richter, R., 936
Rick, J.W., 935
Rigby, J.K., 937
Rinehart, J.S., 874
Ritter, D.F., 50
Robinette, W.L., 426
Robinson, J.T., 938, 939
Rodriguez, J., 940
Rodriguez, W.C., 941, 942
Roe, F.G., 943
Roger, J., 944
Rogers, A.F., 945
Rogers, E.S., 946
Rolfe, W.D.I., 947
Rollins, H.B., 948
Romer, A.S., 949
Ronen, A., 420
Roper, D.C., 950
Roper, M.K., 951
Rose, J.J., 952, 1015, 1020, 1021
Rouse, I., 953
Ruangwit, U., 954
Rubberechts, V., 428
Rudberg, S., 955
Ruddy, F.H., 1155
Runnings, A.L., 956
Ruprecht, A.L., 912
Russell, M.D., 957, 958, 959

Skerlj, B., 1038
Sadek-Kooros, H., 960, 961, 962
Sagan, E., 963
Saha, S., 679
Sampson, C.G., 224
Sanger, D., 141
Sankey, J.H.P., 238
Sather, J.H., 391
Saunders, J.J., 964
Saunders, J.K., 965
Savage, H., 966
Schäfer, W., 967, 968
Scherer, M., 969
Schick, K.D., 206, 970, 971, 972
Schildman, G., 391
Schindel, D.E., 82
Schoeninger, M., 1016
Schoeninger, M.J., 910, 973
Schopf, J.M., 974
Schumann, H., 427
Schumm, S.A., 975
Schwarcz, H.P., 244
Schwartz, H.L., 976
Scott, K., 977, 978
Scott, L., 979
Scott, R.W., 980
Scotter, G.W., 981
Scrivner, P.J., 982
Seidensticker, J., 983
Seilacher, A., 984, 985, 986, 987, 988, 989
Sekulic, R., 990

Semenov, S.A., 991
Sepkoski, J.J., 992
Serventy, D.L., 1081
Shackleford, J.M., 993
Shackley, M.L., 994, 995, 996
Shalimov, A.I., 997
Shannon, J.A., 891
Shchegolev, A.K., 998
Sheppard, P., 864
Sherwood, A.M., 587
Shipman, P.L., 906, 907, 999, 1000, 1001, 1002, 1003, 1004, 1005, 1006, 1007, 1008, 1009, 1010, 1011, 1012, 1013, 1014, 1015, 1016, 1017, 1018, 1019, 1020, 1021, 1022, 1023
Shkurkin, G.V., 480, 481
Shotwell, J.A., 1024, 1025
Shrock, R.R., 1026
Siegfried, W.R., 1027
Sillero-Zubiri, C., 1028
Silvestrini, G., 37
Simmons, N.M., 981
Simons, E.L., 430
Simons, D.B., 1029, 1030, 1031, 1032
Simons, J.W., 1033
Simpson, G.G., 1034
Simpson, S.V., 680
Sinclair, W.J., 1035
Singer, B.H., 448
Singer, R., 521, 1036
Singh, I.B., 931
Sisson, S., 1037
Skinner, J.D., 1039, 1040, 1041, 1042
Sloss, L.L., 663
Smith, A.J., 401
Smith, B.D., 1043
Smith, J.W., 1044
Smith, R.M.H., 1045, 1046
Snyder, S.W., 649
Soffer, O., 456
Solomon, S., 1047
Solorzano, F., 1048
Spencer, B., 1049
Speth, J.D., 1050
Spinage, C.A., 1051
Splingaer, M., 588
Stallibras, S., 1052
Stanford, D., 517, 914, 1053
Stanley, S.M., 917
Stanton, R.J., Jr., 331
Steele, D.G., 1054
Stein, J.K., 1055
Steinfeld, P., 449
Stevens, M.A., 975
Stockton, E.D., 1056
Stoddart, L.C., 1057
Stokes, W.L., 1058
Stone, N.M., 109, 110, 111
Stout, S.D., 1059
Strahler, A.N., 1060
Straus, L.G., 1061, 1062

Sutcliffe, A.J., 1063, 1064, 1065, 1066, 1067, 1068
Swegle, M., 196
Szpunar, C.B., 680

Tamahama, K., 1069
Tanabe, K., 1069
Tang, C., 242
Tanner, D.P., 488
Tappen, N.C., 1070, 1071, 1072, 1073, 1074, 1075, 1076, 1077
Taquet, P., 310
Tarlo, L.B.H., 583
Tasch, P., 1078, 1079
Taylor, D.N., 220
Taylor, J.H., 1080
Tedford, R.H., 1216
Teichert, C., 1081
Thackeray, J.F., 1082
Thiadens, A.J.H., 702
Thijssen, R., 701, 702
Thomas, D.H., 1083
Thomas, G., 1084
Thompson, D.Q., 1085
Thompson, M.E., 241
Thorson, R.M., 327, 1086
Thunen, R.L., 445
Thurman, M.D., 1087
Tilson, R., 523
Tilson, R.L., 1088
Tobias, P.V., 1089, 1090, 1091
Todd, L.C., 112, 1092, 1093
Tomenchuk, J., 92, 1094, 1095
Tomenchuk, S., 1095
Tooby, J., 1096
Toots, H., 556, 856, 857, 858, 1097, 1098, 1099, 1100
Toth, N., 206, 972
Toy, T.J., 1101
Trewin, N.H., 1102
Trinkaus, E., 1103
Trump, T.E., 458
Trusheim, F., 1104
Tsekhovskiy, Yu.G., 1105
Turner, A., 392, 1106, 1107, 1108, 1109, 1110
Turner, C.G., 1111, 1112
Turner, G., 170
Turner, M., 667
Tuzin, D., 190
Tverskaya, L.A., 1212

Ubelaker, D.H., 1113
Uerpmann, H.-P., 1114
Uhlmann, D.R., 585
Urist, M.R., 773

Valentine, J.W., 1115
Valoch, K., 1116
Van Aarde, R.J., 1042
Van Couvering, J.A., 27, 1023
Van Couvering, J.A.H., 27, 1117
van den Bosch, M., 702

Van Der Lingen, G.J., 1118
Van Der Merwe, N.J., 1119
van Dijk, T., 702
Van Frank, R., 949
van Overbeeks, A.P., 701
VanderHoof, V.L., 221
Vas, L., 195
Vaughan, J., 1120
Vehik, S.C., 1121
Verbicky-Todd, E., 1122
Vereshchagin, N.K., 1123, 1124, 1125
Verzilin, N.N., 1126
Veyrier, M., 1127
Visher, G.S., 1128
Voigt, E., 1129
Von Blottnitz, J., 523
Von Endt, D.W., 1130
Voorhies, M.R., 817, 1131, 1132
Vrba, E.S., 1133, 1134, 1135

Wadell, H., 1136
Wagner, E., 1195
Walcott, R.H., 1049
Walker, A.C., 548, 1022, 1023, 1137
Walker, D.N., 418
Walker, K.R., 1138, 1139
Walker, P.L., 1140
Walmsley, R., 1044
Walters, I., 1141, 1142
Warme, J.E., 1143
Washburn, S.L., 1144
Wasmund, E., 1145
Waterridge, L.E.D., 458
Watkins, L.L., 1146
Watson, G.S., 1147
Watson, J.P.N., 1148
Webb, S.D., 360, 418
Weigelt, J., 1149, 1150
Welbourne, R.G., 1151
Welles, S.P., 220, 222, 223
Wells, C., 1152, 1153
Wells, L.H., 1154
Welsh, W., 1102
Weltin, T.P., 348
Wendt, J., 969
Wessen, G., 1155
West, R.M., 719
West, R.R., 980
Western, D., 83, 1156, 1157
Wexlar, D., 337
Wheat, J.B., 1158, 1159, 1160
White, E.M., 1161
White, R., 1162
White, S.E., 1163
White, T.D., 1164, 1165
White, T.E., 1166, 1167, 1168, 1169
Whitham, G.B., 707, 708
Wiesenauer, E., 988
Wild, C.J., 1170
Wilkinson, P.F., 1171

Will, R.T., 142, 1172
Williams, C.T., 520
Williams, P.J., 211
Williams, P.F., 620
Willis, D.G., 1173
Willmore, L.J., 1087
Wilmeth, R., 1174
Wilson, M.C., 1175, 1176
Wilson, V.J., 484, 1177
Wing, S.L., 1178
Witter, D.C., 1179
Wolberg, D.L., 1180, 1181
Wolf, H., 1205
Wolff, R.G., 1182, 1183
Wolman, M.G., 697
Wolpoff, M.H., 1184
Wood, A.E., 1185
Wood, W.R., 1186, 1187, 1188
Woodland, B.G., 1210
Woodward, G.D., 1189
Wright, N.E., 949
Wright, R.V.S., 555
Wright, T., 1190
Wyatt, J.R., 1191
Wyckoff, R.W.G., 309, 310, 329, 330, 384, 993, 1192, 1193, 1194, 1195
Wymer, J.J., 1196

Xiang-Xu, X., 567

Yaalon, D.H., 1197
Yacobaccio, H.D., 1198
Yanagi, G.T., 79, 84
Yanin, B.T., 1199, 1200
Yeager, C.P., 425
Yellen, J.E., 1201
Yesner, D.R., 1202, 1203
Yi, S., 1204
Yochelson, E.L., 1205
You, Y.-Z., 1206
Young, D.E., 1207

Zach, R., 1208
Zachry, D.L., 1210
Zangerl, R., 1209, 1210
Zapfe, H., 1211
Zarkhidze, V.S., 1212
Zeder, M.A., 923, 924
Zegwaard, G., 1213
Zeimens, G.M., 418, 419
Zhang Zehenchun, 863
Ziegler, A.C., 1214
Zierhut, N.W., 1215
Zimmerman, M.R., 1216

Key Word Index

Abrasion
 artifacts, 254, 255, 403, 994, 995, 996
 bones, 199, 319, 331, 360, 369, 566, 645, 652, 653, 781, 803, 842, 901, 1006, 1023
  experimental, 182
  SEM study, 1020
 sand grains
  SEM study, 549
 shells, 146, 331, 347, 348
 stones, 2, 661, 668, 669, 670, 671, 672, 975, 994, 996
Accumulations. See Bone accumulations; Shell accumulations, 1
Acid modification (See also Scats)
 of bone, 134, 627, 966, 1005
  by standing water, 1135
 of insects, 809
 of teeth, 395, 396, 397, 768
Actuopaleontology, 936
 marine
  defined, 968
Anatomy and taphonomy, 1137
Antler
 mechanical properties, 745
Assemblages (See also Mortality)
 life vs. death
  marine, 742, 797, 1143
 life vs.death, 146
  marine, 214
  models, 478
 models of, 601
 types of, 387
Available meat, 475, 477, 724, 1043
Bed forms (See also Hydrology; Sedimentology), 18, 20, 179, 502, 603, 607, 609, 619, 771, 782, 1029, 1030, 1031, 1032
Bibliography
 fossil vertebrates, 216, 217, 218, 219, 220, 221, 222, 223, 479, 480, 481, 505, 506, 949
 of faunal analysis, 723
 taphonomy, 815
Biocoenose, 1145
 defined, 968

Biostratinomy, 813, 985
Bioturbation (See also Pedoturbation; Stratigraphic disturbance)
 marine, 986
Bison, 943
 age determination, 647
Bison kills (See also Mortality, catastrophic), 5, 85, 323, 350, 407, 410, 411, 413, 415, 417, 592, 616, 617, 928, 1050, 1122, 1158, 1159, 1160, 1176
Bone (See also Antler; Ivory)
 color, 186, 467, 1000, 1001, 1016
 density of, 727, 729
 hydraulic equivalent, 652, 653
 mechanical properties, 113, 129, 210, 278, 381, 382, 383, 527, 560, 745, 886, 1044
 physiology, 362, 372, 522, 773, 1120
  cement lines, 679
Bone accumulations (See also Den; Transport)
 causes of, 40, 170, 580, 1110, 1129
Bone dwellings, 456, 654, 885
Bone grease, 95, 692, 1121, 1215
Bone modification. See Acid modification; Burnt bone; Carnivore modification; Gnawing; Hominid modification; Worm modification, 1
Bone tools. See Hominid modification, 1
Bone-bed, redefined, 30
Book review
 Binford, L.R.: Bones, 100, 137, 198, 409, 476, 482, 515, 579, 581, 1172
 Bonnichsen, R.: Pleistocene Bone Technology, 359, 493
 Brain, C.K.: The Hunters or the Hunted?, 351, 437, 640
 Dart, R.A.: The Osteodontokeratic Culture of Australopithecus, 247
 Graham, R.W., J.A.Holman, and P.W. Parmalee: Taphonomy and Paleoecology of the Christensen Bog, 282, 1181
 Klein, R.G., and K. Cruz-Uribe: Analysis of Animal Bones from Archaeological Sites, 180, 705
 Morlan, R.E.: Taphonomy and Archaeology, 359
 Speth, J.D.: Bison Kills and Bone Counts, 108, 441, 703 807, 915

Borings
 bones, 37
  by arthropods, 628
 shells (See also Predation, on mollusks), 184, 422, 790, 940, 1205
Breakage
 antler
  in vivo, 524
 bone (See also Bone, mechanical properties; Fragmentation; Hominid modification; Trampling of bone), 127, 470, 527, 645
  by rock fall, 326
  frozen, 864, 1086
  natural, 4, 673, 842, 957, 972
  patterns, 929
 metal cylinders, 51, 812, 874
 shell, 52, 150, 944, 988, 992, 1102
 size analysis, 1148
Burial
 algae, 650
 artifacts, 324, 823
 bone, 319, 1126
 fish, 794
 organisms, 429, 813
 shell, 454, 600, 684, 854, 1212
 small mammals, 810
 spores and pollen, 655
 types of, 1124
Burnt bone, 143, 433
 cremation, 93, 94, 526, 572, 709, 710, 1087, 1152
 experimental, 196, 1016, 1087, 1152
 histology of, 406, 526
 prehistoric, 1152, 1153
  Australia, 33
  China, 107, 710
  Europe-West, 693
  Malawi, 272, 274
  Peru, 908
  USA, 93, 94, 1112
  USA-Northeast, 325
 pseudo, 186
 SEM study, 1004
 shrinkage of, 572
Burrows. See Stratigraphic disturbance, 1
Butchery (See also Hominid modification)
 ethnographic
  !Kung, 1201
  Athapaskan, 713
  Cree, 946
  Eskimo, 95, 96, 486, 1179
  Kenya, 433, 444
  Kutchin, 850
  Maasai, 762
  Paraguay, 604
  USA, 1166, 1167, 1168, 1169
  USA-Plains, 1122
 experimental, 415, 416, 605, 855, 1053
 historic
  Europe-West, 428
  USA-Northwest, 720

 of baboon, 112, 1012, 1013
 of buffalo, 410, 413, 547, 593, 618, 1050, 1122, 1159, 1186
 of camel, 418
 of caribou, 485, 850, 1179, 1202
 of dugong, 795, 796
 of elephant, 855, 1053
 of hominids, 693
 of llama, 908
 of mammoth, 414, 496, 791, 978, 1054
 of mastodon, 193, 394, 398, 1015
 of sheep, 349
 prehistoric, 102, 246, 535, 722, 733, 918
  Africa-East, 112, 204, 207, 751, 752, 905, 1004, 1012, 1013, 1020, 1164
  Africa-South, 633, 1201
  Australia, 340, 795, 796
  Botswana, 1151
  Canada-West, 349
  Denmark, 835
  Great Plains, 594
  Greenland, 485
  Malawi, 272, 273, 274
  Olduvai, 541
  Peru, 908
  UK, 224, 978
  USA, 547, 1166, 1167, 1168, 1169
  USA-Alaska, 1202
  USA-Michigan, 394, 398
  USA-Montana, 191
  USA-Northeast, 488
  USA-Northwest, 496, 618, 726, 791
  USA-South, 1187
  USA-South Dakota, 450
  USA-Southeast, 389
  USA-Southwest, 1050
  USA-West, 410, 412, 413, 414, 593, 1159, 1186
Butchery sites (See also Bison kills; Kill sites), 631
Calcified bone. See Burnt bone, 1
Calculus, 401
Cannibalism
 ethnographic, 34, 190, 208, 552, 963, 1213
 prehistoric, 951, 1038
  China, 109
  Indonesia, 586
  Krapina, 957, 1103
  UK, 187
  USA-Southwest, 1111, 1112
  USA-West, 826
Carnivore modification (See also Predation; Scavenging), 33, 60, 62, 70, 96, 97, 98, 101, 107, 130, 134, 142, 156, 165, 166, 201, 270, 287, 289, 326, 339, 360, 444, 507, 508, 511, 531, 537, 558, 595, 617, 627, 746, 783, 877, 878, 922, 1000, 1001, 1017, 1018, 1019, 1023, 1054, 1061, 1066, 1144, 1153, 1211
 bear, 512, 513, 514
 canid, 514, 1052, 1176
 cat, large, 514
 crocodile, 354
 dinosaur, 333
 dog, 230, 340, 470, 621, 738, 873, 1141, 1142

fox, 368
hyena, 181, 370, 386, 514, 542, 543, 664, 793, 934, 1039, 1040, 1064
insect, 181, 888, 889, 890
leopard, 1033
lion, 370
of anthropoids, 430
of hominids, 1076
sarcophilus, 59, 315, 343, 716, 717
SEM study, 261, 1007, 1020
shark, 321
thylacinus, 59
Thylacoleo, 1, 315, 316, 317, 452, 555, 1049
wolf, 510, 512, 513, 776
recent, 280
Cave paleontology, 32, 157, 159, 165, 166, 248, 270, 326, 340, 343, 458, 466, 487, 509, 716, 717, 785, 788, 791, 842, 981, 1033, 1061, 1063, 1154
Color. *See* Bone, color, 1
Communications theory, 1078, 1079
Community concept, 602
Community reconstruction, 43, 474
Community structure, 28, 283
Computer analysis. *See* Methodology, faunal, computer, 1
Conference report, 41, 77, 82, 138, 140
Coprocoenosis, 652, 653, 777
Coprolites. *See* Scats, 1
Corrosion. *See* Acid modification, 1
Cremated bone. *See* Burnt bone, 1
Cryoturbation. *See* Frost Action; Pedoturbation, 1
Cutmarks (*See also* Butchery; Hominid modification), 96
experimental, 1140
SEM study, 183, 1005, 1007
history of
Iran, 611
prehistoric, 272
Africa-East, 197, 204, 206, 207, 440, 442, 446, 732, 751, 752, 905, 906, 1009, 1010, 1164, 1165
Africa-South, 168, 274
Canada-West, 1175
Canada-Yukon, 803
Europe, 959
Krapina, 958
SEM study, 197, 199, 201, 261, 901, 959, 1005, 1007, 1009, 1015, 1020, 1021, 1165
UK, 262, 978
USA-Michigan, 398
USA-Southeast, 360
pseudo, 26, 79, 84, 393, 1021
Decomposition, 530, 532, 967, 968, 1149
by bacteria, 88, 1209
by insects, 427, 451, 599, 867, 868, 869, 888, 890, 927, 941
factors of, 65
gases, 1210
of alewives, 322
of bone, 887
of dinosaurs, 333
of dogs, 927
of elephants, 252, 253, 468
of fish, 769

of guinea pigs, 144
of human cadavers, 612, 941, 942, 1146
of lizards, 267
of marine vertebrates, 30
of pigs, 867, 868, 869
of pika scats, 492
of rabbit, 238
of shells, 239, 240, 241, 706
of squirrels, 9
of toads, 267
of ungulates, 550
Den
carnivore, 166, 567, 907, 1033
hyena, 901
hyena (*See also* Hyena behavior), 199, 200, 523, 533, 538, 543, 629, 793, 901, 902, 979, 1014, 1040
Diagenesis (*See also* Fossilization), 57
marine, 11, 58, 559, 822, 969
of bone, 460, 680, 860
Dialectical method, 367
Differential preservation
of bones
archaeological, 109
Differential preservation (*See also* Limb bone ratios)
ethnographic, 762
of birds, 376
of bones, 331, 796
archaeological, 40, 59, 96, 101, 106, 155, 162, 163, 164, 165, 166, 181, 199, 200, 230, 272, 273, 274, 289, 346, 428, 440, 442, 444, 446, 449, 485, 571, 576, 611, 630, 631, 632, 633, 634, 636, 646, 699, 748, 751, 795, 844, 845, 880, 901, 902, 903, 934, 1050, 1109, 1135, 1151, 1158, 1159, 1186, 1187
due to density, 727, 729, 734
ethnographic, 95, 153, 154, 604
human, 1113
paleontological, 43, 69, 149, 245, 318, 319, 432, 491, 545, 566, 584, 629, 645, 685, 688, 689, 917, 999, 1000, 1001, 1006, 1045, 1131, 1132
recent, 70, 83, 153, 319, 530, 574, 1171
of insects, 809
of invertebrates, 30, 257, 331, 361, 700, 765
of phytoliths, 892
of shells, 658, 686, 825
of teeth
paleontological, 645
Digestive acids. *See* Acid modification, 1
Disarticulation (*See also* Butchery), 1045
dinosaurs, 333, 467, 688, 689
fish, 769
insects, 809
mammals, 96, 118, 119, 530, 535, 536, 537, 545, 546, 547, 736, 1099, 1131, 1149
shells, 1102
Ecological diversity, 28
Element counts. *See* Differential preservation, 1
Faunal condensation, 421, 623, 624, 625
Fossil protiens. *See* Fossilization, 1
Fossilization (*See also* Paleohistology; Prefossilization), 364, 365, 467, 558, 1150, 1192

chemical composition, 195, 227, 263, 520, 587, 1097
conditions of, 504, 974
diagenesis, 150, 1080, 1130
histology, 373, 374, 1216
inorganic composition, 945
    iron, 556
    trace elements, 61, 123, 189, 375, 613, 615, 680, 856, 857, 858, 860, 909, 910, 973, 1155
microstructure of, 55, 457, 1192, 1193
of fish, 171
of plants, 851
of wood, 36
organic composition, 264, 499, 1192
    amino acids, 678
    collagen, 328, 329, 583, 678, 865, 993, 1194, 1195
    fatty acids, 308, 384
    lipids, 309
    protein, 310, 330, 1130
process of, 265, 472, 520, 813, 853, 944, 947, 1084, 1209
silicification, 150
Fossils (*See also* Fossilization)
types of, 944
Fracture of bone. *See* Bone, mechanical properties; Breakage; Fragmentation; Hominid modification, 1
Fragmentation (*See also* Bone, mechanical properties; Breakage)
bone, 200, 331, 444, 693
    by plow, 737
    size analysis, 1151
metal cylinders, 51, 812, 874
shells, 331
Frost action (*See also* Pedoturbation; Solifluction), 590, 598, 1163
Gnawing (*See also* Carnivore modification), 1005
by artiodactyls, 23, 134, 379, 452, 463, 591, 990, 1065, 1067, 1068, 1156, 1191
by porcupines, 157, 181, 279, 521
by rodents, 33, 54, 60, 66, 134, 277, 291, 326, 508, 521, 558, 1034, 1035, 1153, 1185
    SEM study, 1020
by sheep, 188
Grain size, 405
History
of paleoecology, 825
of paleontology, 825
of taphonomy, 81, 99, 136, 138, 140, 167, 303, 335, 436, 443, 532, 544, 674, 753, 848, 849, 1091
    Sonderforschungsbereich 53, 525
of vertebrate paleoecology, 849
Hominid modification
prehistoric
    Africa-East, 21
    China, 460
Hominid modification (*See also* Butchery; Cutmarks; Pseudo-tools)
ethnographic, 443, 444
    Africa-East, 433, 434
    Africa-South, 305
    Australia, 465
    Cree, 130, 1215

Eskimo, 95
Paraguay, 604
San, 200
experimental, 91, 127, 130, 142, 204, 311, 470, 596, 754, 804, 855, 961, 962, 1053, 1094, 1207
historic, 991
    Europe, 428, 743, 744
    Iran, 447, 449, 611
prehistoric, 96, 135, 136, 152, 175, 178, 225, 258, 544, 595, 596, 646, 753, 839, 918, 991, 1083
    Africa-East, 76, 104, 120, 199, 201, 202, 204, 206, 207, 433, 434, 440, 442, 530, 531, 532, 642, 691, 770, 901, 903, 905, 1002, 1011, 1017, 1196
    Africa-South, 101, 131, 158, 160, 161, 163, 166, 169, 181, 285, 286, 288, 289, 290, 291, 292, 293, 294, 295, 296, 297, 298, 299, 300, 301, 302, 304, 305, 306, 521, 562, 571, 758, 759, 920, 921, 922, 938, 939, 1089, 1090, 1144, 1180
    Australia, 33, 59, 316, 338, 339, 340, 341, 342, 1049
    Botswana, 1151
    Canada-East, 767
    Canada-West, 622
    China, 6, 7, 14, 75, 107, 109, 110, 111, 116, 145, 173, 176, 242, 303, 516, 568, 681, 714, 715, 731, 779, 843, 876, 877, 933, 1062, 1093, 1184, 1198, 1204, 1206
    Czechoslovakia, 1116
    Denmark, 828, 829, 830, 831, 832, 833, 834, 835
    Europe, 699, 748, 896
    Europe-West, 693
    France, 64, 780, 840
    Great Plains, 594
    Greenland, 676, 799
    Lebanon, 824
    Malaysia, 503
    Mexico, 1048
    Monaco, 177
    New World, 226
    North America, 1203
    Peru, 908
    South America, 192, 558
    Spain, 90, 408, 1127, 1162
    UK, 306, 627, 977, 978
    USA, 919, 1036
    USA-Alaska, 1202
    USA-Great Plains, 416, 1160
    USA-Michigan, 398
    USA-Northwest, 496, 788, 789, 791, 960
    USA-Southeast, 311, 360
    USA-Southwest, 127, 139, 593, 597, 781, 911, 914, 1054
    USA-West, 410, 411, 412, 413, 415, 418, 419, 517
    USSR, 1125
    Venezuela, 953
    Yukon, 132, 133, 134, 500, 501, 573, 610, 802, 803, 806, 808
Hunting. *See* Predation; Scavenging, 1
Hydrology (*See also* Bed forms; Kinematic waves; Paleohydrology; Sedimentology), 19, 179, 502, 608, 619, 682, 695, 697, 782, 1030, 1031, 1032, 1128
Hyena behavior (*See also* Den, Hyena; Scats, hyena), 194, 370, 523, 533, 534, 538, 539, 540, 543, 561, 562, 563, 564,

664, 665, 666, 740, 792, 811, 852, 934, 1014, 1028, 1039, 1040, 1041, 1042, 1088, 1107
Hyena dentition, 385
Hyena scats. *See* Scats, hyena, 1
Ivory
   fracture of, 128
      by elephants, 260
Kill sites (*See also* Bison kills), 95, 631
Kinematic waves, 578, 682, 786
Lair. *See* Den, 1
Limb bone ratios, 119, 202, 901, 902
   of birds, 376
   unit weights, 121
Maceration
   shells, 12
Methodology
   assemblage
      life vs. death, 146
   collagen extraction, 244
   faunal, 141, 159, 234, 237, 258, 268, 346, 389, 636, 725, 728, 766, 845, 870, 925, 1024, 1037, 1082, 1095, 1214
      computer, 251, 276, 439, 643, 763, 764, 775, 923, 924, 1114
      sampling, 39, 65, 67, 231, 245, 249, 495, 872, 1183
      sieving, 871
      similarity, 916
      succession, 1139
      terminology, 235, 753
   fractures, 92, 340, 1095
   geoarchaeology, 455
   geomorphology, 115, 1060
   invertebrates, 1078, 1079
   orientation
      wulff nets, 913
   paleoecology, 431, 687, 980, 1024, 1025
   petrology
      grain size, 405
   photography of bone, 774
   sedimentology, 228, 662, 663, 771, 931, 995, 1136
   SEM, 259, 952, 956, 1003, 1005
   statistical, 243, 275, 1115, 1147
   taphonomy, 548, 815, 1004
   video, 31
Minimum Number of Individuals, 477
Minimum Number of Individuals (*See also* Quantification), 17, 126, 232, 233, 276, 356, 392, 448, 473, 475, 553, 554, 636, 656, 805, 879, 894, 897, 898, 899, 1106, 1108, 1170, 1171
   fish, 895
Mortality, 530, 532, 1109
   attritional, 320, 641, 827
      invertebrates, 937
   catastrophic, 13, 114, 229, 641, 769, 859, 1123, 1125
      alewife, 322
      bison (*See also* Bison kills), 256
      cattle, 626
      causes of, 185
      cervids, 736
      Dall's sheep, 981
      elephants, 260, 266

      elk, 757
      horses, 87
      invertebrates, 657, 937
      marine, 185, 490, 772
      mastodon, 964
      Stenomylus, 711
      ungulates, 550
      walruses, 390
   of bison, 350, 1176
   of fish, 769
   of Irish elk, 56
   patterns of
      living mammals, 236
   types of, 944, 968
   ungulates, 638, 639
      living, 1051
Mummification
   natural, 825, 1149
   of seals, 883
Occupation sites, 631
   vs. kill sites, 636
Orientation, 929, 1147, 1173
   artifacts, 557, 578
   bones, 27, 319, 331, 333, 548, 566, 588, 688, 689, 718, 719, 859, 1000, 1001, 1004, 1006, 1023, 1098, 1100, 1131
   carcasses, 736
   shells, 172, 250, 331, 620, 659, 677, 700, 778, 944, 1026, 1104
      fluvial, 819, 820
   stones, 589, 620, 660
Oryctocenosis, 367
Osteodontokeratic. *See* Hominid modification, prehistoric, Africa-south, 1
Osteophagia. *See* Gnawing, 1
Paleoecology, 70, 78, 367, 1157
   Africa, 253, 577
   Antartica, 577
   East Africa, 1117
   East Turkana, 65, 66, 69, 577
   human evolution, 73
   Morrison Formation U. S. A., 336
   Olduvai, 66
   Omo, 66
   text, 3, 431
   theory, 948
   USA, 469
   USSR, 462
Paleogeomorphology, 115, 755
Paleohistology (*See also* Fossilization), 1059
Paleohydrology, 49, 608, 645, 688, 863, 900, 1128
Pedoturbation (*See also* Frost action; Stratigraphic disturbance; Trampling of bone), 148, 324, 823, 861, 997, 1105, 1188, 1197, 1199
   by ants, 838
   by gophers, 377
   by hooves, 683, 982, 1118
   by rodents, 483
   by termites, 151, 215, 312, 313, 471, 838
   by trilobites, 989
   by worms, 38, 209, 307, 378, 838, 1055

marine, 284, 421, 984, 989, 1026
Pellets (*See also* Scats), 652, 653, 777
  bird, 761
  hawk, 357, 801
  hyena, 60, 1028
  owl, 24, 25, 157, 166, 270, 337, 357, 380, 459, 498, 675, 704, 712, 716, 800, 801, 912, 926
  raptor, 358, 368
  SEM study, 261
Porcupine gnawing. *See* Gnawing, porcupine, 1
Predation (*See also* Pellets; Scavenging), 530, 532
  by *Panthera*
    on macaques, 983
  by bears, 489
  by birds
    on snails, 461
  by carnivores, 118, 665, 903
    on mice, 875
  by cheetahs, 667
  by crocodiles, 395, 396, 397, 768
    on macaques, 425
  by hominids, 118, 404, 582, 637, 641, 977, 1107
    on *Camelops*, 517
  by hyenas, 370, 523, 664, 811
    on equids, 1110
  by leopards, 157, 667
  by lions, 370, 371, 667
    on equids, 1110
  by starfish, 930
  by whelks, 881
  by wild dog, 667
  by wolves, 776, 891
  marine, 968
  on bovids, 1133, 1134
  on dinosaurs, 333
  on hominids (*See also* Cannibalism), 1134
  on jackrabbits, 1057
  on mollusks (*See also* Borings, shells), 790, 930, 988, 1205
  on primates, 22
  on rodents, 25
  on sheep, 528
  social behavior of, 741
  stone age, 635
Prefossilization (*See also* Fossilization), 30, 825, 929, 974
Preservation (*See also* Differential preservation; Fossilization)
  of bone, 464, 499, 575, 648, 1125
  of human skeletons, 453
  of shells, 614, 987, 1069
Pseudo-tools, 152, 186, 622, 690, 730, 736, 817, 821, 1036, 1065
  arguments for, 494
Quantification (*See also* Available meat; Minimum Number of Individuals; Taxonomic diversity)
  of faunal remains, 356, 448, 475, 477
  Rodent burrows. *See* Stratigraphic disturbance, 1
  Rodent modification. *See* Gnawing, by rodents, 1
  Rounding. *See* Abrasion, 1
  Sampling (*See also* Methodology, faunal, sampling)
    artifacts, 403

bias, 231, 748, 871, 976
Scanning Electron Microscope (SEM)
  bone abrasion, 182
  methodology, 952, 1005
  study, 1002, 1137
    bone color, 1016
    bone use-wear, 956
    burnt bone, 1004, 1016
    cutmarks, 26, 183, 197, 199, 206, 261, 262, 906, 1007, 1011, 1015, 1020, 1021
    sand abrasion, 549
    tooth marks, 261
Scats (*See also* Coprocoenosis; Pellets), 777, 929
  bobcat, 426
  carnivore, 652, 653
  coyote, 391, 651, 816, 1085
  crocodile, 395, 396, 397
  fox, 332
  hyena, 60, 1027, 1028
  leopard, 484, 1177
  lynx, 965
  marten, 212
  packrat, 89
  pika, 492
  Sarcophilus, 716
  wolf, 402, 776, 891, 1085
Scattering of bone. *See* Transport, 1
Scavenging (*See also* Predation), 149, 271
  by badgers, 529
  by canids, 1052
  by foxes, 529
  by hominids, 118, 641, 752, 920
  by pigs, 424
  on sheep, 528
  vs. predation
    hominid, 642, 732, 749, 770, 843, 866, 905, 933, 1008, 1009, 1010, 1093, 1096, 1119, 1133, 1134, 1135, 1196
  vs.predation
    hominid, 21, 75, 76, 101, 103, 104, 105, 107, 109, 118, 119, 120, 122, 203, 205, 207, 516, 569
Schlepp effect, 440, 442, 446, 576, 636, 879, 880
Sedimentology (*See also* Bed forms; Hydrology; Kinematic waves; Paleohydrology; Transport, of sediment), 19, 117, 228, 405, 410, 697, 882, 884
Settling velocity, 662, 747
Shell accumulations
  types of, 8
Shotwell's method, 474
Site
  classification, 42, 115
  formation, 403, 433, 434, 435, 465, 604, 1188, 1201
  process of, 438, 970, 971
Size effect, 83, 150, 155, 159, 160, 161, 163, 470
Size frequency distributions, 846
Soil erosion, 694, 696, 698, 750, 1101
  down slope movement, 955
  sheet wash, 719
Soil pH
  bone preservation, 464

Solifluction, 174
Spiral fractures. *See* Hominid modification, 1
Split-line cracks, 954, 1070, 1071, 1072, 1073, 1074, 1075, 1077
Sternburg law, 2
Stratigraphic disturbance (*See also* Frost action; Pedoturbation; Solifluction; Trampling of bone), 32, 215, 438, 551, 823, 861, 935, 1188
    cryoturbation, 211, 269, 570, 585, 654
    dicynodonts, 1046
    earthworms, 29
    gophers, 377
    human, 565, 760, 1056, 1174
    insects, 29, 932
    lungfish, 352, 353
    plowing, 737, 950
    rodents, 125
    size effect, 48
    soil erosion, 750
    termites, 798
Systems theory, 644
Taphonomic feedback, 625
Taphonomy
    analysis and interpretation, 327, 401
    defined, 363, 364, 365, 367, 431, 917
    introductory work, 74, 1092
    models, 63, 142, 469, 644, 686, 721, 1078, 1079
        mortality, 245
    of plankton, 739
    of plant remains, 399, 650, 655, 851, 998, 1105
Taphonomy, history of. *See* History, 1
Taxonomic diversity, 477
Thantocoenose, 1145
Time resolution, 35, 71, 72, 862, 1178
    conference report, 82
Tooth marks. *See* see Gnawing, 1
Trampling of bone (*See also* Stratigraphic disturbance), 26, 27, 70, 79, 84, 433, 435, 438, 444, 513, 517, 548, 683, 817, 842
    by elephants, 260
    by mastodons, 964
    experimental, 393, 445
Transport
    by porcupines, 161
    by runoff creep
        of coarse debris, 314
    fluvial, 2, 46, 47, 67, 69, 124, 149, 213, 245, 284, 319, 331, 333, 334, 355, 364, 365, 388, 434, 438, 467, 497, 545, 574, 578, 588, 649, 652, 653, 707, 708, 719, 787, 803, 818, 968, 976, 1006, 1045, 1104, 1189
    of artifacts, 996
        by animals, 518, 519
        by bower bird, 1047
        by rain wash, 420
        by vultures, 814
        fluvial, 574, 578, 863, 970, 971
    of bedload
        fluvial, 45, 50
    of bone, 32, 80, 566, 580, 688, 689, 929, 1000, 1001
        by ants, 1022

    by birds, 400, 606, 761, 836, 1081, 1141, 1142
    by bower bird, 1047
    by carnivore, 161, 629
    by elephants, 344, 345, 468
    by hillwash, 746
    by hominids, 746
    by hyenas, 161, 287, 523, 533, 534, 538, 540, 561, 562, 563, 564, 746, 793, 1014, 1040, 1064
    by marine currents, 813
    by porcupines, 10, 157, 166, 746
    by river ice, 1086
    by vultures, 814, 893
    fluvial, 46, 47, 65, 67, 69, 124, 149, 245, 319, 331, 334, 364, 365, 369, 434, 438, 467, 497, 545, 574, 588, 652, 653, 719, 803, 813, 847, 863, 968, 976, 1006, 1045, 1131, 1182, 1189
    models of, 1134
    of carcasses
        by floating, 467
    of fossils
        by wind, 1058
    of index fossils, 15, 16
    of organisms, 1200
    of sediment
        fluvial, 44, 787, 837
    of shells
        by birds, 53, 606, 841, 1081, 1190, 1208
        fluvial, 331, 369, 649, 701, 702, 778
        marine, 8, 147, 284, 423, 684, 701, 702, 778, 818, 827, 1102, 1104
    of stones
        fluvial, 2, 388
Trophic analysis, 1138
Urban taphonomy, 447
Use-wear
    on bone, 956
Volcano modification of bones, 730, 736
Weathering
    bone, 30, 68, 70, 86, 152, 164, 181, 199, 245, 281, 319, 435, 438, 531, 558, 595, 784, 803, 885, 901, 904, 964, 1000, 1001, 1005, 1006, 1023, 1071, 1072, 1073, 1074, 1075, 1077, 1161, 1189
    fossil, 65
    hominid fossil, 66
Wolf behavior, 776, 891, 1085
Worked bone. *See* Hominid modification, 1
Worm modification, 558